It is a rare treat for an artist of this caliber to talk to others about his craft in a revealing way, (especially if it's a guitar player). Superstition common to the species dictates that if forbidden secrets are circulated by a master, he'll lose his gig at the local pub.

But in these pages the master architect of jazz guitar takes the apprentice on a guided tour through his workshop, with an easy rhythmic pulse that goes from storytelling to serious shop talk. His toolbox is equipped with concepts like "hearing the pencil," for coaxing musical ideas out of that other dimension and onto the drawing board.

It seems the new age has produced a strain of musical clones that resemble lemmings going happily over the edge. So, for those who wish to break away from the pack, Jim Hall (a guitar player) has designed an escape route to the musical self.

Joff Jones
Guitar Editor
Hal Leonard Publishing

ISBN 978-0-7935-0392-6

© Universal Press Syndicate 1990, All Rights Reserved

Line drawing by Gary Larson
Color rendering by Lavrans Neilsen

7777 W. BLUEMOUND RD. P.O. BOX 13819 MILWAUKEE, WI 53213

Dedication

....

This book is for my wife, Jane.
Much gratitude goes to
three guitar players: Charlie
Christian for inspiring it,
Jeff Jones for polishing it,
and Gary Larson for decorating
it.

Jim Hall
Oct. 12, 1990

Contents

Photo Credit: Jane Hall

Jim Hall

Leonard Feather and Whitney Balliett have compared him to Django Reinhardt and Charlie Christian in stature and influence. Paul Desmond compared him to Pablo Casals. Joachim Berendt described him as "a master of delicate, sensitive guitar improvisations...*the* timeless guitarist par excellence." Sonny Rollins has referred to him as "the greatest guitarist in jazz" and Alec Wilder once wrote of Jim "It is as if he were so marvelously disciplined as to be able to choose his notes from a long accumulated and even hoarded wisdom — that kind of wisdom that is reached by having intelligently absorbed from his whole life experience... His choices of notes seem to be transmitted from memories of joy, misery, mistakes, realizations, humilities and wonderments." What then have been some of the joys, realizations and wonderments in the life of this man that the English call "The Quiet American?"

Jim Hall was born in Buffalo and raised in New York and Ohio. Spending his early years first in New York, then in Columbus and ultimately in Cleveland, Jim was first introduced to music at home by his mother who played piano, his violin-playing grandfather and his uncle who played the guitar. When Jim was 10 years old his mother gave him a guitar for Christmas and it was then that he began to seriously study the instrument. By the age of 13 Jim had become a professional musician playing locally in Cleveland with a group consisting of an accordian, clarinet, drums and, of course, guitar. The clarinet player turned Jim on to Benny Goodman's recording of "Solo Flight" which featured the guitar playing of Charlie Christian. "It was instant addiction" recalls Jim.

It was later that Jim was introduced to the playing of Django Reinhardt by guitar teacher Fred Sharp. Jim continued to play in small combos throughout high school, and after graduation entered the Cleveland Institute of Music where he majored in music theory. Of that time Jim recalls "I played guitar on weekends but wasn't all that involved in jazz. I thought I was going to go into classical composing and teach on the side. Then, halfway through my first semester towards my master's degree, I knew I had to try being a guitarist or else it would trouble me the rest of my life."

Shortly thereafter Jim quit school and made his way across the country to Los Angeles in a lavender Cadillac in the company of friend and fellow musician Ray Graziano. Upon arriving in Los Angeles, Jim lived with his great aunt and worked in a used sheet music store while studying classical guitar with Vicente Gomez. It wasn't long thereafter that Jim met a french horn player by the name of John Graas at the local musician's union who recommended him to Chico Hamilton for his quintet. It was then, in 1955, with Buddy Collette on reeds, Freddie Katz on cello and Carson Smith on bass, that Jim Hall began to attract national, then international, attention.

Jim stayed with Chico's group for one and a half years. During that time there were several trips back to the East Coast to play at Newport and in New York. During one particular engagement, playing opposite Max Roach's group at Basin Street, Jim first met Sonny Rollins with whom he was to later work. In 1957, after leaving Chico's group, Jim joined Jimmy Giuffre's trio, originally with bassist Ralph Pena, then bassist Jim Atlas and finally trombonist Bobby Brookmeyer. "Giuffre's idea — at least after Brookmeyer joined us — was to have three linear instruments improvise collectively," recalls Jim. "He believed it didn't make any difference whether or not the group had bass or drums. He said the instruments should be able to keep time themselves. It was damn hard, yet it was one of the most enlarging experiences I've had."

Jim left the Giuffre trio briefly to tour Europe and South America with both Yves Montand and Ella Fitzgerald. It was while on tour in South America with Ella Fitzgerald that Jim, engrossed with the "local" music, left the tour to spend six weeks in Rio de Janeiro just as the Bossa Nova was coming into being. This exposure was to prove invaluable and become a part of Jim's musical versatility as evidenced later in his recordings with Sonny Rollins ("What's New" - Victor 1962) and Paul Desmond ("Take Ten" - RCA 1963 and "Bossa Antigua" - RCA 1963.)

Upon his return to the states, Jim rejoined the Jimmy Giuffre trio and stayed until 1959 when he moved back to the West Coast. Back in Los Angeles Jim worked with his own combos as well as with Ben Webster's group with Jimmy Rowles on piano, Red Mitchell on Bass, and Frank Butler on drums. It was also during this period that Jim made his first musical contact with pianist Bill Evans and recorded "Undercurrent" (United Artists 1959). Throughout the '50s Jim was active in the recording studios working with such jazz greats as Hampton Hawes, Bobby Brookmeyer, John Lewis, Zoot Sims, Paul Desmond, Lee Konitz, and, of course, Jimmy Giuffre and Chico Hamilton.

In the early '60s, prompted by friend and fellow musician John Lewis, Jim moved back to New York City where he worked in a duo with Konitz. In 1961 came what Jim looks back on as the turning point in his career. Sonny Rollins, just coming out of a two-year retirement, asked Jim to join his group with Walter Perkins and Bobby Cranshaw. They stayed together for a little over a year, rehearsing afternoons at the old Five Spot. Of that year Jim recalls "He (Sonny Rollins) had a way of taking a tune apart and putting it back together again right in front of your eyes...his loose and adventuresome way of playing influenced my playing."

Jim continued to tour and record throughout the early '60s working frequently with Art Farmer, bassist Steve Swallow and drummer Pete LaRoca, as well as with Lee Konitz, Bill Evans, Paul Desmond, Stan Getz, Sonny Stitt, Helen Merrill, Red Mitchell, and Zoot Sims. In 1965, weary of the road, Jim decided to give up touring for awhile.

He got married, settled in New York City and joined the Merv Griffin Show orchestra. Three and a half years later Jim left the Griffin Show ready to tour the club and concert circuit once again, this time leading his own groups. The late '60s saw Jim quite active on the circuit as well as recording with Gerry Mulligan, Quincy Jones and Herbie Hancock, and touring Europe too.

In the '70s, Jim pursued several diverse creative settings. He recorded with free-jazz saxophonist Ornette Coleman. Then, no stranger to duo playing, Jim entered into partnerships with a number of bassists including Ron Carter, Red Mitchell, Jack Six, Harvie Swartz, Jay Leonhart and Michael Moore. Performances of two of these duo groups have been captured on recordings: three albums with Ron Carter, first on a Milestone release entitled "Alone Together" (1972) and then in the '80s "Live at the Village West" and "Telephone" both on Concord Records; and with Red Mitchell an album simply entitled "Jim Hall/Red Mitchell" recorded live at Sweet Basil in New York City (Artists House 1978).

Recordings in the '70s have included "Concierto" (CTI 1975) featuring bassist Ron Carter, saxophonist Paul Desmond, trumpeter Chet Baker and pianist Roland Hanna, with one entire side of the LP dedicated to Don Sebesky's arrangement of the adagio movement of Jocquin Rodrigo's "Concierto De Aranjuez." In 1975 the trio recording "Jim Hall Live" with drummer Terry Clarke and bassist/pianist Don Thompson was also released. The trio was expanded in 1976 to record the A&M/Horizon album entitled "Commitment" featuring Art Farmer and Tommy Flanagan. Shortly thereafter the trio made a tour of Japan where they recorded two albums "Live In Toykyo" and "Jazz Impressions of Japan" (A&M/Horizon and Artists House) the latter featuring all original material.

During the last few years Jim has continued to be very active and still pursues more new avenues of musical expression. In addition to performing a commissioned work by Bobby Brookmeyer with the Stockholm Radio Symphony funded by the Swedish government, and playing on two jazz oriented albums featuring violin virtuoso Itzhak Perlman and concert pianist/conductor Andre Previn, Jim also recorded four other albums. Three of these were on Concord Records, "Circles" with Thompson and Clarke, "First Edition" a duo album with pianist George Shearing, and "Three" with Steve LaSpina on bass and Akira Tana on drums. The fourth album, entitled "Power of Three", on Blue Note Records with Michael Petrucciani on piano and Wayne Shorter on saxophone, was recorded live at the Montreax Jazz Festival.

On June 26, 1990 the JVC Jazz Festival honored Jim with a Town Hall Concert called "The Jim Hall Invitational." Jim performed in duets with Ron Carter, Bob Brookmeyer, Gerry Mulligan and Pat Metheny. He also played with Gary

Burton and Don Thompson in several pieces (by Hall, Thompson and Piazolla) featuring a string ensemble; and with his own quartet featuring Gil Goldstein, piano, Steve LaSpina, bass and Terry Clarke, drums. Guitarists John Ambercrombie, Peter Bernstein, Mick Goodrick and John Scofield joined Jim on the second half of the concert. All of this was recorded live by Music Masters.

When not busy recording, playing clubs or touring, Jim devotes a great deal of time to composing, practicing and teaching...looking for new ways to express himself through his music and to share those expressions with others. When asked by Guitar Player magazine if he was very self-critical, Jim replied "I am, but I do feel good about my playing. The instrument keeps me humble. Sometimes I pick it up and it seems to say 'No, you can't play today.' I keep at it anyway, though."

by Devra Hall

Magic Meeting

It's 8:30 a.m. and I'm in our house in the woods. It's winter and there's snow. The house is mostly glass. It's set into a hillside so it feels like a tree house. I'm wondering what's in the woods. Many possibilities: deer, squirrel, grouse, any kind of song bird that hasn't migrated. Quite a few hawks around; even eagles, I've been told.

This is the time, that special time when everything is fresh and undiscovered. This is the "magic meeting" time. One wants to treat it gently, with respect and intelligence.

The first time I saw Duke Ellington's band felt like this. The Palace Theater in Cleveland, Ohio in the early 1940s. The afternoon movie finished and the audience got real quiet. Darkness in the theater. You could hear a few instruments warming up behind the heavy curtain. I had never seen Duke's band — had seen hardly any music performed, in fact. I had never met a famous musician. Then we heard a piano play a few chords and the saxophones hit the first low G of "Take The A Train." The thick, red curtain opened and there was the band. Almost. The surprises weren't finished. The musicians still had a light, gauzy, scrim curtain in front of them. You could see their outlines and the lights from some of the music stands. An occasional reflection off of a horn. Magic! A magic meeting. The music was great. After a while (I don't know how many choruses) the scrim lifted and there they were — Duke Ellington and his famous orchestra! I was probably thirteen or fourteen years old and I don't remember what music they played or who was in the band. (I'm sure there were famous people and a beautiful lady singer.) What I do remember are those first moments of hearing and then seeing the band from a seat in the darkened Palace Theater. What an experience. What a rare and lovely experience.

I draw on that experience often when I'm approaching a performance. There's an audience out there that hasn't yet heard anything. They've neither been won over nor alienated, although one can assume most of them are there because they want to be. They're friendly toward you. They're on your side. If you succeed, then they do as well and the evening has been a success. The first sounds they hear can effect what happens, the player/listener relationship, for quite a way into the performance; perhaps the whole way.

The image of the glass house in the woods is involved here, too. What's outside is unknown. What music is to be heard is unknown. What the characters in a play are going to do or say is unknown, until they reveal themselves to the audience. This is the one magic moment that's given to us; it's free and to be used with care.

Self-Expression

In the late 1950s John Lewis put together The School of Jazz at the Music Inn in Lenox, Massachusetts. For several years, we convened, or converged, for three weeks late in the summer and had quite an impressive line-up of faculty, as well as students. At the close of one of these summer sessions, we had a student/faculty meeting and John Lewis was speaking to all of us in a sort of fatherly, serious, but encouraging way, about what we had accomplished in three weeks and about some of the remarkable new things that were happening in jazz.

A couple of the students weren't buying this and started anxiously questioning John: "Are there any gigs out there?" "What's the pay off?" "Can I make enough money with jazz so that I don't have to take a day job?" John endured this for quite a while and then said, perhaps over-dramatically, "Wait a minute! You've got it backwards. Being able to play jazz is your reward. There is no other pay-off."

Obviously I'm paraphrasing after so many years, but it's a point well taken. The ability to play music, and especially to improvise music, is the finest reward to be gotten from all of this and seems especially pertinent today, thirty years later. In this era, when young peoples' educations are so often aimed at something practical or business-like (being competitive with the Japanese or not letting the Russians get ahead of us), here is a chance to have something for yourself; here is a way to express what *you* are. Just knowing what music is and how it works gives you inside rewards: a feeling for the balance of things, an appreciation of the hard work of others and empathy because music is hard. Music is also a powerful way of influencing people, convincing them, getting a feeling or an attitude across to others and immersing them in it for awhile: "Here, try this. See how it feels."

You do have something to sell people in a sense and the details are up to you. Is what you're selling beneficial? Is it in their interest, yours, or both? Is it cheap? An illusion? A deceit? Will it enrich them and you? If it won't do this last thing, at least in intent, then I hope you will find something besides music to sell. We're already overcrowded with the other. The opportunity to perform in public and make money at it is a sort of bonus, a privilege. It can disappear quickly, often with no obvious reason, the same way it appeared.

If you go into music only with an eye toward "making it" you're missing the main point and you'll probably not receive the inside, personal rewards that are unique to this art form.

I've made some recordings which have sold well. Often, the more popular ones are not my favorites, but I have never done a recording specifically for commercial reasons. I've always figured that salability would be a by-product of having made something truly good: a recording with some content. Besides, while calculatedly commercial records may get hot and sell a lot for a few months or a year, a really class jazz record will be in demand forever. Having integrity isn't all self-denial. Self-expression can pay-off, too.

There are record shops where one can find recordings from practically the beginning of jazz. After all, recording and jazz sort of grew up together. In Japan, I was taken to a store where I found my first recording as a leader ("Jim Hall, Jazz Guitar"), long since out of print in this country. The Japanese had made beautiful pressings of it and had reproduced the original cover, so they weren't just old, scratchy copies. What a joy! Also there were lots of hard to find Ben Webster, Art Tatum and Tal Farlow records and there were people in the store buying them. The invention of the compact disc is also helping this process of not allowing good recordings to disappear.

The point is this: when I make a record, the money gets spent fast but the record is there forever. Why not make it a good one? Why not use it to express myself? Why not communicate something decent?

Preparation: Mental

You may find, as I do, that it's sometimes necessary to talk one's self into performing well. If I'm feeling particularly rattled and not confident right before show time, I'll take some deep breaths and tell myself that for the next hour or so I am *the star*. Even if I don't really believe it, I've got to be that for the audience; they believe it enough to spend their money and they deserve as good a performance as I can muster. They really do. (I can be depressed on my own time.)

Nothing can be more rattling than not knowing what we're going to play. I always have a program plan and even if I change it on the stage, it's comforting to have. It relieves me of the pressure of having to think of the next tune while performing. You've all heard those terrible silences while the musicians ask each other "what do you want to play?", and the audience begins to ask itself "who cares?"

A typical set plan may contain five tunes and should have a definite shape to it. I usually think of the opening tune first, then the last tune. A slow tune (perhaps a ballad) could proceed the last tune. Then I work out the other two, maybe a blues plus a medium tempo.

The first tune is very important. It's the first sound the audience is going to hear and it should work appropriately for you: an attention-getting ear-catcher. This doesn't mean it has to be fast and "show-offy," but it could be. Remember the "Magic Meeting."

Concentration is a big factor in my performing well, especially since I'm not a virtuoso guitarist, and I rely on being tuned in to what is happening around me. This concentration process starts well before the first note is played, continues as the music starts and I get more and more sensitized to the other musicians. It reaches its highest plane when I can play anything that needs to be played with my eyes closed—never looking at the guitar fingerboard. At that point, I'm really a part of the music.

Before work, I try not to hear any music; it can be distracting and confusing. Listening to Pat Martino tapes for an hour may make me love Pat Martino's playing, but it's also liable to discourage Jim Hall the guitar player and he's the one who's getting paid to play today.

I try to get myself quiet and meditative wherever I am: hotel room, band room, or even taxi cab if the driver's not trying to have an accident. This is another reason to head for the work place early.

I read that before a match, Billie Jean King would roll a tennis ball around the floor of her room and concentrate on watching it, shutting out everything else. That's the kind of process I'm trying to describe.

On the other hand, talking with your fellow musicians can be a help because it starts the unifying process that's going to continue through the playing. Also, humor is a great relaxer and unifier and can really draw people together, which is where they need to be to play music.

Once the music starts, my concentration works its way through the band, usually beginning with the bass and continuing upward through the drummer's cymbals. The string bass gets my attention early, since I hear it as a downward extension of the guitar, as well as the low end of the overall texture. All of my chord voicings are influenced by what the bass plays (and, I hope, visa-versa) and my single lines may go different places depending on what I hear the bass doing.

From there on it's a process of interacting; listening, trusting, and reacting.

In all of this, awareness seems to be the key word —hearing, or seeing the music from one step outside, looking down from above.

As you play, divide your time between being observer and participant, as you would when writing music. Recreate the best possible composition situation. After all, improvising is instant composition.

Preparation: Physical

I am a big fan of hot water. If I can get my hands warmed-up and all of the parts stretched loose and comfortable, I stand a pretty good chance of performing well even after a hectic trip with little warm-up time. Practicing right before "hit-time" has mostly to do with confidence anyway; I want to reassure myself about my feel for the guitar strings. Moderately hot water helps me. It brings back a comfortable feeling to hands that may have been numbed by lifting amplifiers and/or driving for several hours. I remember talking about this with Bill Evans at Café Bohemia. He used to warm up in a variety of ways (subject to availability): by running hot water on his hands; holding them under an electric hand drier, or the tried and true hands-folded-under-the-armpits method.

This is one of the reasons I try to arrive early at a gig; I want to be well rid of the road before the first downbeat.

Athletes do the same thing and for the same reasons, I imagine. They want to be warmed-up, relaxed, play well, and not get injured. For musicians, the injuries are mostly narcissistic, although physical hurts can happen, too.

Pro tennis players often arrive at a tournament site a few days early to get used to the court surface — speed, bounce, etc. — and the general ambiance. Being a tennis fan, I take a lot of cues from these people.

If I'm starting an overseas tour, I'll often get there a day or two early to get rid of jet-lag and make sure all my equipment survived the plane trip. I'll also do some muscle-stretching in the hotel room every day and try to aim my concentration toward the first performance, not unlike a tennis player. I do, however, avoid throwing my guitar down in anger whenever possible.

Careful

By James S. Hall

"Careful" - Explored

The joke I always make about this piece is that it's called "Careful" because it's a 16-bar blues and that, if you're not careful, it becomes a 12-bar blues. Actually, the first 3 notes suggested the words "Be Careful" to me:

"Be Care-ful..." but I never finished the lyric, or any other lyric, for that matter. I sometimes wonder whether Beethoven had a lyric in mind for his Fifth Symphony; maybe something light, like:

Of course it would have been in German, but why not? Anyway, "Careful" was written in 1958 as a Thelonius Monk-type blues for the quartet led by my then employer and still good friend, Jim Giuffre, who played it on tenor saxophone. Since then, I have recorded it with Gary Burton and George Shearing. It has evolved into an even-8th-note (as opposed to loose-triplety-8th note), middle-eastern sounding piece. I refer to it as a "Greek blues." Years ago, there was a 16-bar blues called "Soft Winds,"* which was recorded by the Art Tatum/Tiny Grimes/Slam Stewart Trio among others. It was my harmonic model for "Careful."

The "Be Careful" motive is scattered about through the tune like this. This is denoted by the use of a ⌐‾⌐.

The basic intervals involved are an augmented 2nd and a major 3rd:

In bar 13, there is a quickened version of the motive with a major 2nd and a major 3rd:

Beats one and two of bar 14 have even closer intervals:

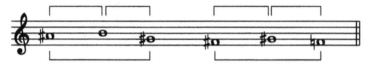

and it may be stretching things a bit to consider this the "Be Careful" motive. It does however come back on the last beat of bar 14 and the first two beats of bar 15:

One can also look at the tune this way — in four note groupings:

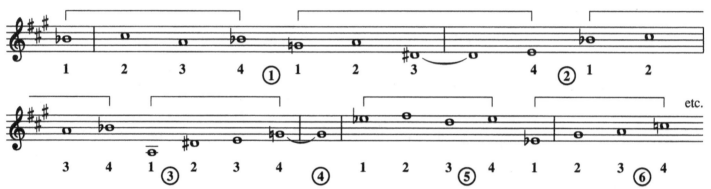

The main point is that the piece is *constructed* with some *logical order* and this same logic can be applied to improvised solos. Also, "Careful" is built on the 8-tone diminished scale that Dizzy Gillespie and John Coltrane explored so thoroughly:

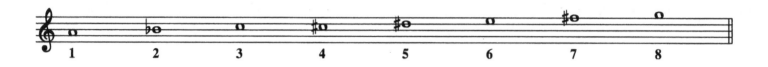

With a slightly different spelling, we can extract two diminished 7th chords from this scale a minor 2nd apart:

A Diminished 7th   B♭ Diminished 7th

We also have some nice melodic interval possibilities:

I've made some enharmonic spellings to keep all the intervals minor 3rds...

(The numbers above the staff refer to scale degree)

Major thirds:

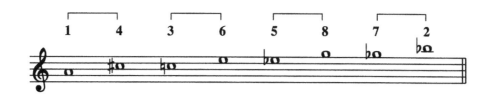

Here are combinations of augmented 4ths and diminished 5ths;

again with funny spellings:

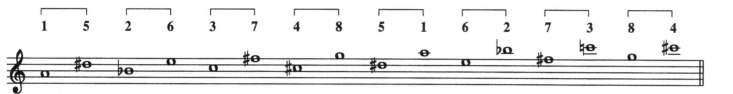

Here is a sequence of perfect 5ths followed by augmented 5ths, or minor 6ths, depending on the spelling..

This example gives us major 3rds, followed by perfect 4ths. Again, I've bent the spellings a bit. Also, don't forget that this scale has an extra note in it. It's an 8-tone scale, nine if we repeat the "A" at the octave..

Major 6ths are inverted minor 3rds. While they give us a nice symmetry on the fingerboard, the major 6ths again require slight note-spelling adjustments in order to keep the intervals accurate....

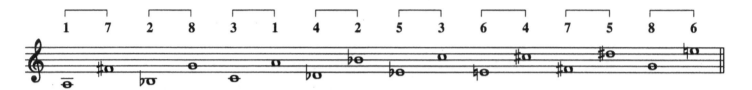

D♭ to B♭ is a major 6th...

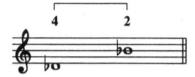

C♯ to B♭ is a diminished 7th, even though they sound the same.

This next example gives us an interesting sequence of minor 7ths followed by major 7ths:

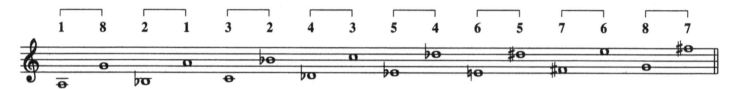

If we continue this exploration process and look at the triadic possibilities, we come up with this:

all diminished triads

Here's a sequence of minor and major triads:

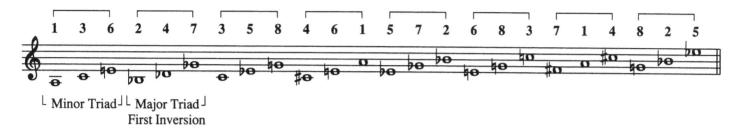

| 1 | 3 | 6 | 2 | 4 | 7 | 3 | 5 | 8 | 4 | 6 | 1 | 5 | 7 | 2 | 6 | 8 | 3 | 7 | 1 | 4 | 8 | 2 | 5 |

L Minor Triad J L Major Triad J
First Inversion

Now a minor seventh chord, and then a first inversion of a major triad with an augmented 9th on top.

| 1 | 3 | 6 | 8 | 2 | 4 | 7 | 1 | 3 | 5 | 8 | 2 | 4 | 6 | 1 | 3 |

These are fun to play over an open A pedal point:

etc.

I think that's enough information on this. The trick is to make music out of it.

*"Soft Winds" was also the name of a wonderful trio put together by guitarist Herb Ellis, pianist Lou Carter and John Frigo, who played violin and bass. The three of them had been together on Jimmy Dorsey's Big Band (which was where I first heard Herb Ellis) and decided to pool their talents in a trio setting. They also wrote some tunes together including "Detour Ahead," which became very popular.

Music Notation

Music notation should be a matter of friendly co-operation between the writer and the player, with each giving the other the benefit of the doubt on occasion. There is no absolutely perfect way to notate music of which I'm aware. The possibilities for musical nuance and subtlety are infinite and the whole process seems to require a certain degree of camaraderie: "We all want this to be good. Let's try to understand each other."

Since music is really an aural art form, playing a phrase or a piece of music for another musician is the quickest way to have it understood, although that's not sure-fire either. One runs into the problem of human memory. Often I can't remember my own music unless I write it down. Putting ideas or pieces on cassette is helpful and I'm told certain computerized devices can save energy. I haven't yet worked with computers and/or synthesizers, so you'll have to look elsewhere for help with this stuff. My main writing contact is with pencil and manuscript paper, so I try to "hear" the pencil. For me writing music is like problem solving or doing a crossword puzzle. It's much the same as improvising with some differences: there's always a chance to make it better, which can either be an advantage or a terrible trap. Sometimes I just can't let a phrase go until I've fixed and worried all the life out of it. Then, other times pencil notation is a blessing; I can tinker with a phrase or a tune until it's balanced just the way I want it, like a model airplane that flies perfectly. The best is when it comes out right the first time. That's great! Then you have what amounts to improvisation on paper.

Of course, when you're dealing with longer forms or large groups of musicians, some sort of notation is necessary and some kind of mutual understanding of the notation is required. For instance, the first section of my tune "Cross Court" looks like this on paper:

The feeling I wanted was more like this:

However, the triplet notation looks very busy on the page and still isn't completely accurate. It also isn't necessary, since jazz musicians have some sort of agreement about how to play 8th notes. What I did was to write these instructions in the upper left corner of the page and everything worked out fine:

 (rolling triplets)

Jazz musicians also understand "ghost notes" in parenthesis like the ones I used in "Careful"...

...as well as the dot over the B♭...

...the bend over the C♯...

...and the straight line under the A.

In jazz notation, these signs mean, in order; short, bent, and long. The "ghost note" is understood (or should be) as a sort of rhythmic bump, with the rhythm being more important than the pitch. All of these interpretations change with the times and are still changing. The same is true of classical music notation. The rhythms of Bach are played quite differently from those of Delius or Debussy.

Here are the opening measures of the string quartet in G minor by Claude Debussy:

And here are 8 bars of a Bouree for cello by J.S. Bach:

Each of these pieces represent different musical languages, or at least different musical dialects. Without some extra knowledge of the times and the culture in which it was written it is difficult to know exactly what the composer meant.

The Alban Berg "Lyric Suite" was composed in 1926. It has these directions:

"H means principal voice, ending with the mark ⌐

N means second voice, ending with the mark ⌐

⌐ means that the marked part is played in the same rhythm (forming chords) as the principal (H) or second (N) voice, which must, however, be allowed to stand out. The remainder must be kept back as an accompaniment."

The first movement of the "Lyric Suite" is marked *allegretto gioviale,* moving joyfully, which tells us how Berg heard the music regardless of how our ears perceive it. I'm sure his hope was that our perceptions would catch up to his conception.

And this from the foreword to Bach's "The Art of the Fugue," adapted for string quartet by Roy Harris:

"Choice of tempo is somewhat affected by personal preference. Without always being on the slow side, we favor giving room for the singing, articulated discourse of voices. With Bach, the A*lla Breve* sign ¢ is no indication of a doubled tempo (Purcell and others describe it as a 'little faster' than C; it was Quantz who called it twice as fast). Moreover, he seems to have been quite inconsistent in his use of ¢ or **C**. Thus, in each fugue, the determining factor must be found in the music itself."

As you can see from all this, music notation and interest in it have been evolving for a long time...helping others to interpret and perform your music, or, more basically, getting your musical thoughts on paper so that there's an accurate record of them. There is a tradition of using Italian shorthand for many of the instructions (*p, f, espressivo, lento, vivace),* but Debussy wrote his first directions in French: "Animé et trés décide" (animated and very confident, decided). Most composers use a mixture of their own language plus the standard Italian signs. Charles Ives wrote directions in English and some of them are very funny as well as helpful. He had an imaginary effete musician named Rollo at whom he aimed barbed remarks ("hit it, Rollo!") which were probably also meant for hostile audiences.

To me, it's very fascinating and touching to look through music for the composer's directions. It gives one a close look at the intracacies of human communication: "How can I get this on paper so that it will be understood forever?" It also points up the cross-cultural quality of music; you don't have to be Hungarian to feel and understand the opening of Bela Bartók's String Quartet #1. It's marked *lento* ♪=50 *p molto espress.*(very expressively) and it doesn't need translating. You can feel it!

When I was in music school, Bartók was my hero. I was also influenced by various 12-tone composers, including Alban Berg. Recently, in looking at my own string quartet (the only one, so far) I came across this section where I seem to have mashed Bartók and jazz together (possibly also Stravinsky's, "A Soldier's Tale") and come up with some sort of bent tango — this was years before I went to Argentina.

Allegretto Gioviále ♪ = 208

I even thought it should be moving joyfully (*Allegretto Gioviále)*, the same as Berg's "Lyric Suite". So you can see how Italian musical terminology got passed from one non-Italian to another — Vienna, Austria to Cleveland, Ohio.

Looking through a book of George and Ira Gershwin tunes turned up these directions, all of them helpful and some really defining the essence of the song.

- "The Man I Love" (*molto semplice e dolce*-very simply and sweetly)
- "Oh, Lady Be Good" (slow and gracefully). The song isn't often done this way, but it does help make sense of the words.
- "Embraceable You" (rhythmically, but not fast). Charlie Parker recorded it this way.
- "I Got Rhythm" (With abandon). This is one I really like. It makes me think of Ethel Merman singing it!
- "Summertime" has the marking *andantino e simplice* —moving along easily and simply — above the introduction. When the melody starts it's marked *Moderato (with expression)*.

Indications like these do help a performer get the essence of the music, while not being really specific about phrasing, volume and speed. They are exactly the type of thing that a composer will say at a rehearsal, although a jazz writer's vocabulary is a bit earthier and usually not in Italian: "move it!" "hit it!" "groove!" "funky!" "loose swing!" "behind the beat!" "heavy back beat!" "blues changes!" "rhythm changes!" etc... Once again — "We all want this to be good. Let's try to understand each other!"

All Across The City

By James S. Hall

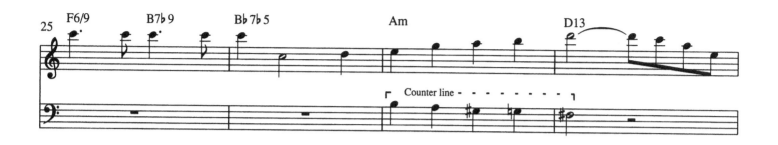

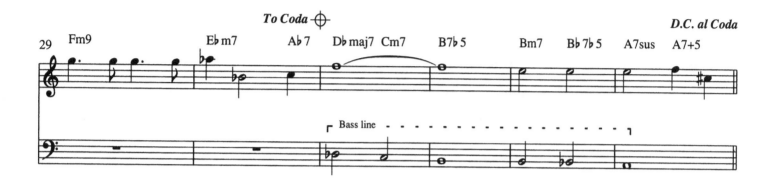

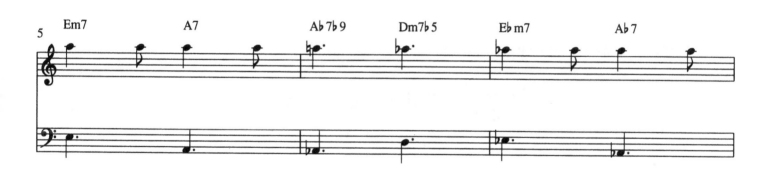

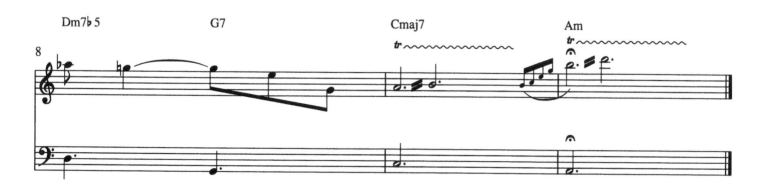

"All Across The City" - Explored

I wrote this tune in 1962, or there about, for a record date with Zoot Sims and Jimmy Raney. It was Jimmy's record and he chose to include another guitar player — me — plus Zoot, Osie Johnson on drums and Steve Swallow on bass. Jim Raney was, and is, one of my best friends and was helpful in getting me used to New York City. He, Zoot and I had been doing a lot of late night jam session playing in various artist's or musician's lofts and the idea for the record grew naturally from that. I guess the title and the mood of the piece had to do with my feelings about the city and I could hear Zoot playing the melody. The original version (the one on this record) had an FmMaj7 chord on the downbeat of bar 4.

I don't like this because there's no difference between the altered F minor chord and the E7 chord, except the F in the bass, which sounds like an accented passing tone to the low E (I've left out the 5th of both chords). By the time I recorded it with Bill Evans (1966), the F minor had become an F dominant 7th with an added 6th, which has more tones to resolve to the E7. This makes a nicer pull toward the AmMaj7 in bar 5.

In playing it through now, I find I prefer the FmMaj7 unresolved, going directly to AmMaj7:

It has a poignant, icy quality to it (not unlike New York) and it makes the AmMaj7 in bar 5 less expected.

Also, measures 10-16 were tricky to harmonize. I liked the Bmaj7 in measure 15 with the D♯ in the melody, but how to get there?

I tried this:

I didn't like the chord pattern repeating symmetrically every measure, nor the Bb7 and Ab7 landing with roots doubled in the melody. I prefer them with the b9 in the melody as they are. The coda also uses this material in a quickened version.

One final word on this piece: it modulates to Db major at the end, and I felt that a two measure extension helped bring it back to the A7 at bar 34 in a comfortable way.

Preparing For A Record Date

In some ways preparing for a record date is the opposite of preparing for a concert. Even though there are usually chances for at least a few "takes" on a record date, often there is not time to get really familiar with the material beforehand. Also, doing take after take sometimes has a diminishing-returns effect; you start to lose your perspective and the piece starts to die on the vine. Many times a take which may have seemed awful at the time sounds surprisingly good after a night's rest. Things like mood and judgement are affected by long hours in a studio.

If I have newly-composed music, it's important for me to have a clear idea of how I would like it to sound, while staying flexible at the same time. I have to be willing to turn it over to the players at some point and to trust them. They will develop a feeling for the piece too, sometimes fresher than mine. Also, being improvisers, they're used to going on their feelings for the moment. This is really important, even if it doesn't precisely match what I thought I wanted. Part of the reason I hired these people in the first place was that I trusted them and liked their playing. It's important that I continue to nurture this trust feeling so that it's in full bloom during the recording. The other players should feel responsible for the music, too. They're not just working a record date for Jim Hall, they're making an important contribution to it and with luck, advancing their own careers. In jazz music, all the players get mentioned on the album and, often, talked about when it's played on the radio as well as reviewed by the press.

Playing in a club or during a concert, I'll often call out ideas as they occur to me: "Play two, Steve!", "Drums and guitar!", "I have it," etc. I like this approach because it allows things to happen spontaneously; it permits things to effect other things and be reacted to. It even permits mistakes to be made and either used or set right. If other things are going well, a dropped beat here or there isn't the end of the world. In fact, it's sometimes a sign that things *are* going well; players are stretching and trying for new ideas and sometimes missing. Good musicians will get back together in a hurry and probably even find it amusing.

On a record date, I may not have quite as much tolerance for slippage and looseness, and hollering out instructions during a take on a recording probably won't go over too well with my producer, although Charles Mingus did this and more. I did a record called "Live At Bourbon Street" where Terry Clarke, Don Thompson, and I got apart a couple of times. It remains just about my favorite J.H. record though, partly because of this looseness. Don Thompson actually made the recording as well as having played beautifully on it. We were working at Bourbon Street in Toronto for two weeks and Don had his recording equipment on the bandstand for most of that time. We got used to it and finally forgot it was there. There's even a sort of comedy-waltz version of Jerome Kern's "The Way You Look Tonight" which ends with a hillbilly A Major chord and a lot of laughter. Would that all recordings were this relaxed. Of course Don and Terry's beautiful musicianship allowed this to happen. A good example of my having hired the right guys!

Simple Samba

By James S. Hall

Something Tells Me

By Jane Herbert Hall

Coda

o Harm.

"Something Tells Me" – Explored: Melody & Accompaniment

Intro: suggests melodic rhythm in G major...

...a major 3rd above the starting Eb major tonality of the melody.

It also establishes the harmonic device of descending 3rds over a pedal point. This device is used a lot in the accompaniment.

In Bar 1 a sudden key change leads us to the melody starting on Eb major: root of G major becomes 3rd and melody note.

(It's not clear whether Eb major is actually the key or the IV Chord of Bb major, the eventual key of the melody.)

Measure 1 of the accompaniment uses an ascending line in contrast to the descending 3rds of the intro. This also leads the way harmonically, providing a sort of cushion through the various tonal centers of the first 8 bars.

Bars 3 and 4 are a sequence of the first two bars.; a perfect imitation a minor 3rd lower.

The 4ths on the first two beats of bar 5 in the accompaniment anticipate 4ths in the melody. Bar 6 continues to use the ascending accompaniment line.

Bars 7 and 8 are a quickened version of the intro. The melody rests on the major 3rd and the harmony descends under it in quarter notes.

This relationship to the intro continues into bar 9. A quick tonality change takes us into B♭ major, which is a major 3rd below D major. This is the same harmonic relationship as between the Intro and Bar 1 of the melody.

In Bars 9 and 10 the melody has settled in B♭ major — a fresh tonality — and the accompaniment continues the ascending line motive. (5, +5, 6).

In bars 11-16, the melody develops and moves a little, while the accompaniment is merely supportive, using the basic harmonies.

Here the melodic rhythm starts with two pickups into the phrase and the accompaniment starts on the second beat (bar 17) to answer it. This is the opposite of the previous pattern.

Bar 19 has two nice dissonances (guitar sounds an octave lower): diminished 8va and minor 9th. Neither of these resolve, but rather ignore the accompaniment.

The harmony here feels like an A major triad against B♭ major triad. It makes a nice tension and is best explained as a B♭ diminished scale:

It's a treatment of the tonic chord which delays the resolution even while defining it. It can probably be traced back to the first caveman's song.

Bars 21-24 wander around through Fm7 (21), Dm7 (22), C7 (23), and some sort of disguised V chord (bar 24) with one of the accompanying lines keeping up the "Something Tells Me" rhythm always following and answering the melody.

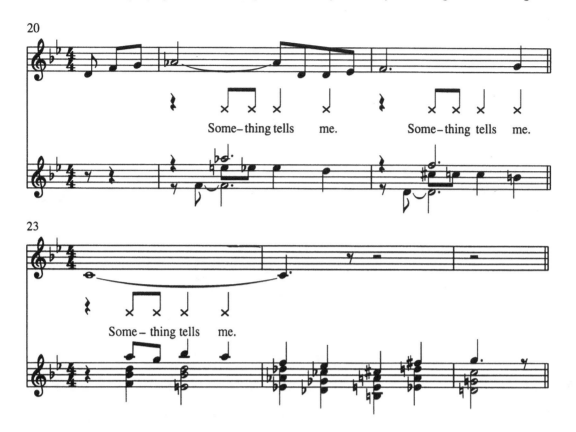

Bar 24 is a sort of tangled-up V chord (a deceptive cadence) and presents an interesting choice of flats or sharps in the chord spellings. It's worth a look...

The flats preserve the look of the intervals. The distance between C♯ and F doesn't look like a major 3rd even though it sounds like one. It's a diminished 4th.

The 2nd beat moves everything down a major 2nd.

On the third beat I switched to sharps and naturals, even though the melodic intervals between beats 2 and 3 look weird; they look like diminished 3rds, but are in a descending major 2nd sequence.

Using sharps here also avoids the use of a double flat which actually doesn't look too off-putting now that I've written it.

However, it does make a strange visual connection to the 4th beat.

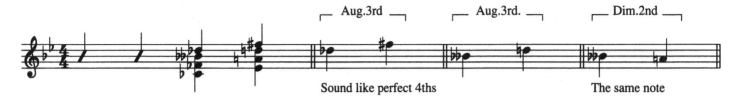

That was a "can of worms" spelling-wise and this looks better:

Having said all this, the use of flats on the 3rd beat does make musical sense, since the first 3 beats are related musically. They're part of the same idea, while beat 4 really connects to the first beat of bar 25.

There's probably no definitive answer to this. It's most likely a matter of choice, but you should at least know what the questions are. This is also strongly related to improvising and the way in which ideas connect! In general, sharps want to pull up and flats want to push down. Talking and writing about flats and sharps (linear note spellings and chord spellings) may seem like an intellectual exercise — a brain game. It is, however, a window that gives us a view of your musicality. If you came to me for guitar lessons, we'd spend a lot of time on these things, probably more time than we would on how to hold your right hand. Left hand fingerings and right hand picking are related to these same musical concerns. Choices of fingerings have less to do with convenience than with where a musical idea is going. How should it sound and where is its arrival point?

Bars 25-28 are a reflection of bars 9-12 with a slightly different windup — an E♮ half diminished 7th (or maybe a C9th with the root omitted). The melody is now set up for a final 8-bar conclusion. The accompaniment uses a descending line for a change. This makes a fresh counterpoint to the melody and works itself downward from the 7th of the B♭ chord in bar 25 to the root of the E∅7 chord in bar 28.

In Bar 29, the melody begins its final spinning out — a lovely sort of quasi-classical section, mostly quarter notes on the beat with the accompaniment following suit.

This type of accompaniment can sound contrived or pretentious if it's overdone. Here we bail out just in time for both the melody and accompaniment to land on their feet. Also, I like the chord on the third beat of bar 34. It's the fullest chord in the piece and it's arrived at smoothly.

The downbeat of bar 35 is an open guitar voicing that seems to work here.

It is a suspension of some sort resulting from bar 34 and thins down to this voicing which sets up the coda:

At the coda we have another sudden key change, this time with an overlap. What would normally be the last note of the melody and the non-existent bar 36 becomes the first note of the coda. The 5th of B♭ major becomes the 3rd of D♭ major:

In the coda, the accompaniment uses the introduction material again in an ostinato manner, while the melody does a fantasy on the first two bars of the tune, starting on various D♭-related chord tones. There are some clashes here, but I think it works. The accompaniment just isn't going anywhere and thus becomes a sort of blank wall or a dark background which will accept anything. There is a quick flirtation with A major in bars 9 and 10, but the piece ends on D♭ — a sort of barren D♭— with no 3rd until the last moment.

Solo Construction:
Some Random Thoughts

Look for ideas and inspiration in other art forms: novels (Marquez, Morrison), short stories (Poe, O. Henry, Thurber), poetry (T.S. Eliot, Roethke), painting (Turner, Monet, Miro, Klee, deKooning, Rothko), cartoons (Price, Thurber, Steinberg, Booth, Larson). These are some of my sources.

When you look at or listen to music there is a natural tendency to imitate. It is helpful to look at things other than music for inspiration.

Go for the shape or the feeling: the form.

A solo is more than playing the right scale against the correct chord. It must have content; inner meaning.

Musical scales, technique, information, equipment, etc., can be like a pile of stones on the ground. Architecture lifts stones off the ground and presents them in an exciting form, made more exciting by our knowing that the stones really want to fall back to the ground.

Think of the "magic meeting" idea again. You are presented with a pile of rocks. You have the opportunity to construct something with them — a free standing stone wall or maybe an archway in a wall.

The wall is the easier of the two (aside from the rock-lifting) because it involves finding rocks that fit one another to form the wall, big ones on the bottom, smaller ones toward the top.

An arch is a different matter. It has tension and drama and contains the possibility that it may fall on itself, fall to the ground and become a pile of rocks again.

Chance taking, and sometimes missing is a big part of the fun of improvising; taking the chance that your solo may fall in on itself, just like the arch of the stone mason. That has happened to all of us at one time or another, and needs to happen more frequently.

Here we're talking about improvisational soloing; basically single line and usually with accompaniment. However, the principles apply to unaccompanied playing as well; it all has to do with composition.

Let's look at some of the words we've used:

construct (Webster's) - 1. to make or form by combining parts: build 2. to set in logical order.

content - 1a. something contained b. the topics or matter treated in a written work 2a. substance. gist b. essential meaning: significance c. the events, physical detail, and information in a work of art.

composition - arrangement into proper proportion or relation and especially into artistic form.

form (Oxford American)- 1. the shape of something, its outward or visible appearance 2. its structure.

Knowing the words to a song is helpful to me. It helps make an improvisation on "Body and Soul" different from one on "Tea for Two."

One ideal is to build a melodic solo that is as good, or better than, the melody on which you're improvising. Paul Desmond was great at this. His recordings are filled with moments where his own incredibly strong melodic sense (improvised) rose well above that of the original composer.

Ben Webster could play just the melody to a standard tune — especially a ballad — in such a way as to make that melody really memorable. Ben had a way of playing just the right notes in just the right places and separating them with just the right silences, tantalizing pauses.

Listen to:
Sonny Rollins "St. Thomas"
Johnny Hodges (with Frank Sinatra & Duke Ellington): "Indian Summer"
Paul Desmond: "I Get A Kick Out Of You"
Charlie Christian (with Benny Goodman): "Solo Flight," "Grand Slam," "I Found A New Baby"
Ben Webster (with Oscar Peterson): "In The Wee, Small Hours Of The Morning"

"Big Blues" - Explored

Improvising coherently involves imagining music appropriately and playing it an instant later. For a guitarist, the main prerequisite is *hearing* the instrument accutely. What pitches are where on the guitar and what musical character does each string and each area of the fingerboard produce?

To help with this sensitizing process, I often experiment by playing the same music on various strings and with a variety of fingerings. I've chosen a 12 bar tune called "Big Blues" to illustrate.

One String Playing: **"Big Blues" On The "D" String**

In bar 1, the 3rd finger gets a nice fat sound on the A♭ and assures a break between the A♭ and the F, unless you have a very large hand. Playing the C♭ with the little finger gives it a bit of nasal edge, which I like. Admittedly, all of these fingerings are arbitrary and often what I say about them is a matter of opinion. Sometimes there's really no choice about fingering, since you're limited to one string. Try limiting the number of fingers too, all the way down to one finger.

In bar 2, you're playing the A♭ and the F with the 3rd and 1st fingers again. This puts the hand in a good position to connect B♭ and F with the 4th and 1st fingers. I have to have my thumb behind the 5th fret to make a rocking motion here:

In bar 3, I've played the repeated "F"s with the 3rd and the 1st fingers so that the two "F"s are separated and sound different from one another. Also, lifting the first finger off the tied-over F makes a little breath before the repeated notes; each of the three F's is different. In bar 5, the octave jump down is probably easiest with 4 to 1, but you might want to experiment with 3 - 1, 2 - 1, and 1 - 1. The A♭ to B♭ I've played by sliding the third finger because I like the sound of it and it's the first slide-slur we've used:

In bar 6, we can't use the original "ghost note" C so we have to make the D short, probably by touching the open string with the 1st finger of the left hand, since it's about to play the F anyway.

This involves a little dance step where the 1st finger first touches the D string lightly at the 3rd fret, just enough to stop it, and then goes on to play the F on the 3rd fret. Playing the A♭ with the 2nd finger adds a little variety since it's the first time we've used the 2nd finger.

In bar 7, I play the next two A♭'s with 3 and 1, so that there's air between them and also between them and the 2nd finger A♭ in bar 6.

In bar 9, the minor 3rd E♭ to C:

is played with 3 and 1. It matches the minor 3rd A♭ to F in bar 1:

I've chosen to play C♭ to B♭:

with 2 and 1 because it's easy and because my hand wants to be ready to move upward for the rest of the phrase.

In bar 10, the fingering for C, E♭, F:

matches the fingering in bar 5:

and also helps move the hand up the neck for the rest of the phrase.

In bar 11, the hand continues upward by lifting the 3rd finger and playing the next F with the 1st finger

In bar 12, I've played the B♭ with the 3rd finger because it's already close by and the 4th finger is just too tricky to get up there.

Again, these fingerings are all arbitrary and may not fit your hand at all. They are arrived at because of the direction of the phrase and the physical motion of the hand. Different fingerings do get different musical results, as you'll see if you experiment.

Sometimes playing "Big Blues" I use all downstrokes in my picking. Also the piece sounds nice played with the thumb.

However you choose to finger it, this exercise is guaranteed to help you get the D string in your ears and under your hand from top to bottom.

"Big Blues" On Two Adjacent Strings: "D" and "A"

Just a word about the repeated notes in bars 3 and 7. "Big Blues" was inspired by Stanley Turrentine's tenor saxophone playing. Each of the repeated notes is meant to have a different sound, like "false fingering" repeated notes on the tenor sax. (Lester Young did this great!) Duke Ellington's brass sections also used this open and closed effect, "doo-wah," with mutes in and out. The "ghost" notes in parentheses are meant to be just little rhythmic bumps to set up the following note. The pitch isn't as important as the effect. If you emphasize a "ghost" note, you'll spoil the effect.

"Big Blues" On Two Non-Adjacent Strings ("G" and "A")

These fingerings are mostly for fun, although they will teach you something about phrasing and nuance on the guitar fingerboard. At least, *I l*earned something from working them out. For instance, the fingering for the last 2 beats of bar 2 helped me to keep the "ghost" note short because I had to move my hand down quickly to the B♭ on the 3rd string.

Again, the main point is to hear and feel the guitar fingerboard...to have it in your senses.

Waltz New

By James S. Hall

⋅_ = separated, but stressed

"Waltz New" - Explored

It's helpful to look at this piece as an improvisation on "Someday My Prince Will Come," even though it took several days to write and is a bit stiff and premeditated—sounding to be an improvisation. With the development of the material, and the direction the line takes, it makes a good model for an improvised solo.

I consider the basic motive of the piece to be a three-note group:

presented in lots of permutations:

and...

The phrase really divides into these groups which move across the barline.

It also breaks down into 2-note groups:

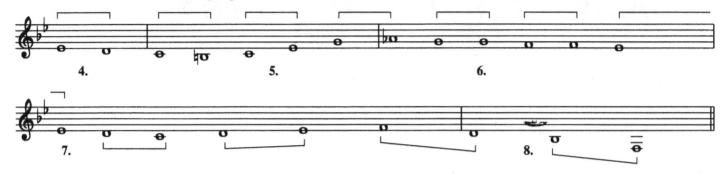

In the next phrase intervals keep expanding:

This phrase gets a running start, goes through a quick modulation, and doesn't stop until bar 18:

It's interesting how welcome the 8th note rest is in bar 18. This points up the importance of space — silence — in music. If one is really involved in the line — really hearing it, singing it, and feeling it, one really needs a breath by bar 18. Two breaths, in fact, and the breaths become longer and more frequent as we go toward the two beat rest in bar 24.

These breaths, these silences are important for the listener as well as the player. Space helps the listener; it gives one's audience a quick chance to reflect on the music, keep it organized in its mental computer, and not get bored or overwhelmed. The listener may just tune out otherwise.

This group is in B♭ major...

and this answering group sounds in C♭ major:

15.

Both are related to bar 1, as are bars 17 and 18:

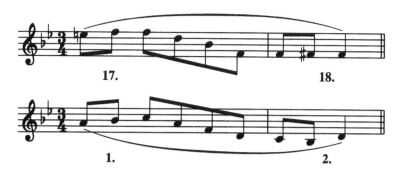

17.   18.

1.   2.

As I recall it was tricky to write the quick C♭ major section (bars 14 and 15) with a single line, but I think it worked out pretty well. The best examples of single line melodies moving through chord changes that I've heard are to be found in Bach's "Sonatas And Partitas" for solo violin and in his six Cello Suites. Charlie Parker wasn't bad at this either, and before him, Coleman Hawkins and Don Byas. The art (and it really is an art) of playing a convincing, musical line through chord changes is well worth cultivating. If you can manage to produce a good melody while you're at it, then you're really traveling in select company—you're hanging out with Lester Young and Charlie Christian. Paul Desmond was also great at this, as I've mentioned elsewhere.

Measures 18 and 19

18.   19.

are a continuation of this idea...

17.   18.

and lead to this...

19.   20.   21.

...then to this...

22.

...and, finally this.

22.   23.   24.

It's all really one long phrase; one sentence which examines itself as it goes along:

This then resolves to the highest note of the piece

and the whole thing unwinds downward to a final suggestion of the first motive from bars 1 and 2.

To sum up, all of this material is related. That gives it cohesion, the same unity that makes a jazz solo memorable.

Chorale and Dance

By James S. Hall

Chorale

* I've written this on two staves for visual clarity and to show the voice-leading. It is all to be played by one guitarist and involves some right hand fingerpicking. Thinking ♩♫♩ sub-divisions keeps it moving.

Dance

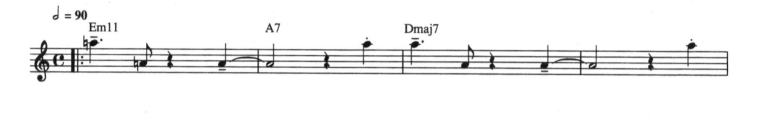

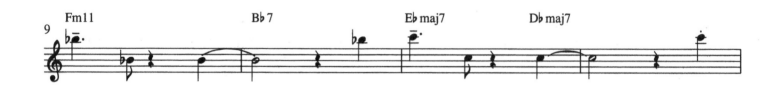

* Improvising on this "Dance" section is easiest with some sort of rhythmic background.

"Chorale & Dance" – Explored

This piece started out as just a chorale; a slow moving, quasi-church like,

A minor melody inspired by Dizzy Gillespie's "Con Alma."

To this, I added a bass line and some implied chord symbols in keeping with a church-like mood:

F♭maj 7 is a rather unfriendly-looking chord spelling, especially since the piece starts in A minor, but I couldn't very well have A♭ being the 3rd of an E major chord. An alternative would have been this:

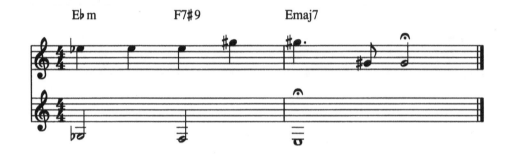

Rhythm Guitar

If playing rhythm ever becomes a lost art, a lot of the fun will have gone out of being a guitarist. Playing four quarter notes to a bar in a good rhythm section is truly a lovely way to spend an evening and probably the closest thing to dancing with a good dance partner. It's like jogging on a beautiful beach or swimming in a warm pool. It gets rid of frown lines.

Freddie Green

When I was in my 20s, I tried to pattern my life after Freddie Green. During my hours on the road behind the wheel of the Jimmy Giuffre Three Volkswagen van, I used to think "how can I make my driving like Freddie Green's playing?" Comfortable, no bumps, pleasant. His playing makes you smile. It also made you *play*, judging by the way Count Basie's band sounded all those years. I once heard the band without Freddie, who was sick. Boy, did they miss him! That great Basie band was like a ship without a rudder. It just wasn't the same.

Freddie once told me that his biggest joy was playing behind Lester Young, who returned the compliment by playing all of those classic solos with the Basie band. I sometimes have a fantasy that, if the tree of jazz were pruned down far enough, we'd be left with just Freddie Green strumming away and making you feel like playing and smiling. After all, Charlie Christian and Charlie Parker heard Lester Young, who heard Freddie Green, etc. etc.

I'll always regret that I didn't watch Freddie more closely or ask him more specific questions about his playing. I did ask Freddie once if he had any fatherly advice for me and he said, "Yes, always pack your bag the night before and leave your uniform on top." I've already described what I felt from his playing. What I heard was something very simple and spacious: chord voicings that allowed the guitar to speak and yet not bump into other rhythm section instruments. For instance, a simple chord progression (III, VI, II, V, I) at a medium tempo in G major might sound like this:

Whether he was playing more notes, I can't say, but this was the effect and, with his magnificent time feeling, it was perfect. It allowed the bass plenty of room to move:

Basie's piano playing never got in the way of anything either. That's a subject for another whole book!

Django Reinhardt

Django Reinhardt was different, in every sense of the word. He was more of a rhythmic agitator, an explorer, who also held the double threat of being able to solo everyone else into bad health — a sort of combination Art Blakey and Sonny Rollins. He played rhythm very much like a good drummer. At a slow tempo, he would sometimes use a chord tremolo the way a drummer uses a snare drum roll; it had the effect of creating dramatic tension and sustaining the harmonies. He used every effect imaginable behind a soloist, including harmonics. Django must have been incredible to play with!

George Van Eps

All of these people must be heard to be believed, but maybe George Van Eps more than any of the others. George is so much more than a rhythm player; he weaves a beautiful tapestry for soloists. It's a musical fabric filled with exquisitely logical voice leadings and stunning surprises. His playing sounds a bit like a distillation of Art Tatum's left hand. He has a fearless harmonic sense, and can find his way out of the most remote musical corner imaginable.

Van Eps comes from a tradition of acoustic, piano-style rhythm playing and I still think of him this way even though he now uses an amplifier. Probably the best insight into Van Eps' playing can be had by looking through his own instruction books — there are several years worth of material in them. Here's an idea of how George might play through these same simple III, VI, II, V, I chord changes:

These examples may be a bit too busy for accompaniments, but they do represent George Van Eps as I hear him. Try them with an even 8th note feeling, like Bix Beiderbecke.

Carl Kress

Carl Kress recorded with Bix Beiderbecke and Frankie Trumbauer in 1927. He also was featured with Paul Whiteman's Orchestra during that same period. He made some famous duet recordings with Eddie Lang and with Dick McDonough. Much later, after years of New York studio work, he joined talents with George Barnes, with whom he also made some terrific records. Carl had his own tuning—unique as far as I know—which included a low B♭ string and looked like this:

Carl Kress Tuning

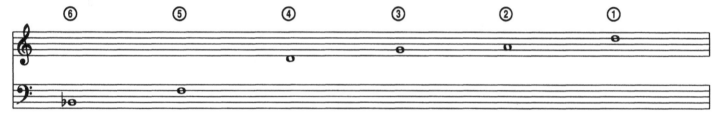

As you can imagine, anyone who could deal with a guitar tuned like this had to be a little different. I understand it grew out of a tenor banjo tuning and just the open strings sound great. Try to play it, though; it's a can of worms!

You can imagine what kind of chord voicings he could get with that 10th spread between the 6th and the 4th strings and the major 2nd interval between the 3rd and the 2nd strings.

I had the honor of knowing and playing with George Barnes and Carl Kress. To know them was a joy! They were both extremely bright and funny and almost as well known for their *bon mots* as they were for their playing. One late night jam session at George's apartment included them playing every tune imaginable on every sort of guitar imaginable and ended with George and Zoot Sims locked in a deadly chess game until daylight... Zoot won.

Allan Reuss

Allan Ruess is another great acoustic rhythm player who was very well known during the big band days. He had some solo spots with the Benny Goodman Orchestra, if my memory is correct, but was mainly, and most important, a part of the rhythm section.

Charlie Christian

Charlie Christian was my first hero. He doesn't really need anymore written about him, except that he's sometimes overlooked as a rhythm player. It sounds to me as if he played rhythm guitar with light amplification and that does seem logical, although with Goodman's Big Band, he may have had two instruments, one for solo and one for rhythm. A number of guitarists did this after amplification became popular. Amplified rhythm just isn't the same as acousitc rhythm (more about this later), especially in a big band.

Barry Galbraith

At a time when most of us guitar players could read chord symbols and that was about all, Barry Galbraith was a real stand-out. I'm not sure what Barry's full background was and how he arrived at his exceptional musicianship. I first heard him with the great Claude Thornhill Band in the 1940s, where he was a part of a perfect rhythm section consisting of Billy Exiner on drums and Joe Shulman on bass and where he also played amplified solos (Gil Evans was the arranger). By the time I met Barry in New York in the mid 1950s, he was on his way to being probably the most recorded guitar player in history because he could do everything. Anything that was required at a record date-single line reading, rhythm playing, accompanying a singer, anything—Barry could do it and beautifully. He recorded some impossibly difficult music of George Russell's (I know because I tried to play it) on some classic records with Art Farmer, Bill Evans, Max Roach, and John Coltrane. He also played simple but perfect acoustic rhythm guitar on all of the Elgart Brothers Big Band recordings. He was an important teacher and a much loved man, a real standout who doesn't get talked about enough.

Billy Bauer

Billy Bauer is another guitarist who played rhythm and solos in a big band. Not just any band, Woody Herman's incredible band—the one before the "Four Brother's" Band—the band that had Dave Tough, Chubby Jackson and Ralph Burns in the rhythm section. The band that recorded "Bijou" and "Caldonia" and "Happiness Is Just A Thing Called Joe" and Igor Stravinsky's "Ebony Concerto." It was an improvising big band and Billy was a very important part of it, an essential color. Later on, he made some landmark records with Lennie Tristano, Lee Konitz and Warne Marsh. Billy Bauer is a real link between the big bands and the avant-garde.

Mundell Lowe

Mundell Lowe is in Southern California now, writing and conducting film scores among many other things. Mundell was a part of Ray McKinley's Orchestra in the 1940s and was featured on some very difficult music that Eddie Sauter wrote. Later, when Eddie teamed with the legendary Bill Finegan to form the Sauter - Finegan Orchestra, Mundell went along. Here he was in a musical setting that was a constant challenge as well as a joy. Eddie and Bill moved jazz band writing ahead by light years, there's no other way to say it, and Mundell was involved while it happened. (So was Barry Galbraith, who made most of the Sauter-Finegan recordings. Barry seems to have been everywhere, as I've already mentioned.)

Oscar Moore

During the 1940s, Nat "King" Cole had a piano, bass and electric guitar trio that had the rare distinction of being a high level musical group and popular with the public at the same time. Oscar Moore was Nat's guitarist for many years, and what a superb, tasty player he was. Oscar had a talent for playing just the right chord voicings to blend with the piano or to set off one of Nat Cole's vocals. He also played very intricate single line parts with the piano (listen to their version of "Sweet Georgia Brown"). His distinctive and memorable solos helped the trio swing as maybe no other trio has. Irving Ashby and John Collins played guitar with Nat Cole later on. Both were outstanding players, and John Collins is still recording and teaching in California. Oscar Moore is the one I remember best though, especially since the "King Cole Trio" inspired a blossoming of piano, bass and electric guitar trios all over the country, even in the backwaters of Cleveland, Oscar Peterson's trio was shaped in this same mold, although it was far more intense than Nat's trios. The first time I heard Oscar's trio, Irving Ashby was playing electric guitar, Oscar was singing a-la Nat Cole, and Ray Brown was playing bass. Later, Barney Kessel took Irving's place, and finally Herb Ellis took over and stayed with Oscar for years. Herb's rhythm playing is just sensational and the combination of him, Oscar Peterson, and Ray Brown was, at times, almost too exciting to bear. I heard them a lot. It was a great, great trio.

Barney Kessel

Barney Kessel is difficult to categorize, and it may be surprising to see his name in a section on rhythm guitar playing. Barney is one of the most important guitarists ever. He's a regular guitar ambassador. He has a rare combination of charm, wit, and talent that makes him an excellent teacher and spokesman for jazz as well as one of its most accomplished practitioners.

I first saw Barney with Artie Shaw's band in the 1940s. It was at the Palace Theater in Cleveland (the same place I heard Duke Ellington's orchestra) and he was using two guitars: an acoustic one for rhythm and an electric guitar for solos. Barney soloed with the full band (I learned his solo on "September Song" when I was a kid) and with the small group the "Gramercy Five." This group, which took its' name from a telephone prefix in New York City, was actually a sextet ("Artie Shaw and His Gramercy Five") and included Roy Eldridge on trumpet and Dodo Marmarosa on piano. I'm sure all of their recordings have been reissued by now and you can hear for yourself what outstanding musicians were involved. Barney had known Charlie Christian and, to my young ears, was sort of an extension of him.

To Amp Or Not To Amp...

I mentioned that amplified rhythm playing just isn't the same as acoustic and that's obviously true. I don't really like to hear electric rhythm in a big band, not even amplified bass and especially not a solid-body bass. Electric rhythm playing seems to clutter the texture of a big band. It gets in the way. On the other hand, in a small group, quartet, trio, or duo — it can work really well. The advantages that the amp gives are that it makes it possible to comp behind a soloist or to hook up with the bass player and play rhythm as a unit (tastefully, I hope). Also if you're working with a pianist, the two of you should be in friendly agreement about who does what and when. I now work in a quartet with pianist Gil Goldstein, and somehow we're able to co-exist. It does take careful listening to each other, though. (There's that word "listening", again.) Often, during a bass solo, I'll play almost acoustic rhythm. This lets the bass be heard easily, gives the drummer a rest if he wishes, and adds a different, softer texture to the music. It's much easier on the bass player too, since all of his nuances can be heard without his having to over-play, and it still gives him something to react to. The piano can get involved or not, as the player sees fit.

Brazil

I can't close out a section on rhythm guitar without mentioning the Brazilians. Some of the best music in the past 20 years has come from Brazil. It's had a big impact on jazz generally and on guitar playing in particular. It seems everyone in Brazil can play the guitar and, with a tradition like this, it's no wonder such miraculous things have happened. Brazil is probably the most musical place I have ever visited. Music is everywhere. It's in the language and in the way people move. It seems to be coming out of the air. Brazilian guitarists play a different musical dialect from that of more traditional jazz guitarists and it would be foolish of me to try to analyze it. I can only recommend that you listen to it. Listen to the compositions of Heitor Villa-Lobos and Egberto Gismonti and everything else in between, from street sambas to bossa nova. Listen to the way Joao Gilberto and Antonio Carlos Jobim accompany themselves. Listen to Laurindo Almeida and to Gismonti's incredible guitar fantasies. Brazilian music is enchanting and Brazilian guitar playing is a big part of the enchantment. Listen to it!

Richie Havens

Finally in a special category, I'd like to mention Richie Havens. Richie has long been one of my favorite rhythm guitar players, although I'm not sure he wants to be thought of this way. Maybe it's because initially Richie stayed away from single note playing and that allowed him time to develop his great rhythmic facility. Whatever it is, I admire it. I also admire Richie as a spokesman for humanity, but it's his rhythm playing that first got my attention. Listen to Richie, it'll make you smile.

Three

By James S. Hall

"Three" – Explored

"Three" -Guitar and String Bass Accompaniment to Flute Melody

The idea of this is to show that one need not use the whole guitar all of the time —a point I seem to make often in different contexts. The accompaniment starts off sparsely with the guitar staying away from both the melody notes and the bass notes. Also, the voice leading (done with the guitars' two notes) is paid attention to and, in time (Bars 37-50) develops into a little counter-melody of its own.

The texture fattens a bit toward Bar 13, where the top note gets into a 10th relationship with the melody. The guitar is still away from the bass (no roots of chords on the bottom) and under the melody. In the ten bar section Bars 17-26 I've used the open "G" string as a kind of drone device and to create tension. My favorite spot here happens in Bar 24. At Bar 27 the texture thins out again, with the guitar playing a little Viennese waltz horn part. The fact that the 4-part guitar settings are abandoned here can be looked upon as a change in orchestration —a good concept for accompanying in any case.

The texture thickens again toward Bar 35 and then as the melody begins to run out of steam, the guitar becomes an equal partner in the melodic chores, leading to the F♭ major 7th with trilled notes (Bars 50 and 51). I realize this is a rather uncommon chord spelling, and it may be a bit hard to "see" at first, but it seems the correct one to me. An E major 7th here would have left the flute to deal with a well entrenched E♭ while the others were toying with D sharps, C sharps, etc., an even stranger looking situation and since seeing is believing, one that would surely disturb the players' ears as well.

This 55 bars of three-part music took me most of a day to write out, so one would hardly call it improvised. (I wish I could improvise something this clearly). It does, however, point out some very important improvising considerations: mainly, clarity of texture and an alertness to the form (the shape) of the piece. The catch is, of course, that three people wouldn't improvise in exactly this way, so that in real life, all of the actions and reactions would be different. This, then, is a make-believe, never-never-land presentation, but one worth studying, (otherwise I wouldn't have taken the day to put it on paper!).

A Look At The First 16 Bars of the Melody

Features:

Scale-wise, downward motion imitated.

Harmonically stagnant dominant with tonic pedal.

Last F in melody retains suspended feeling.

Original melody

Melodic contour of original melody

Target pitches (destination points of melody)

"F" is the remembered note (throughout example)

Bar 5 repeats Bar 1. Bar 6 imitates higher, expands downward intervals but ends on the same F.

Bars 8-10 imitate bars 6-7 with expanded downward intervals, B♭ enters early as an elision, phrase comes to rest late (bar 9) and a new note (G♭) is introduced.

Bar 11 imitates Bar 1 a major 3rd lower. Phrase starts in middle of 4-bar pattern where other phrases had been at rest.

These patterns are repeated and varied throughout the 55 bars of the melody: the scale-wise downward 3 note groups and the upward, chordal groups of 4 quarter notes.

The whole thing has a nice continuity to it. Again, it's something to keep in mind as it applies to successful improvising.

Cross Court

By James S. Hall

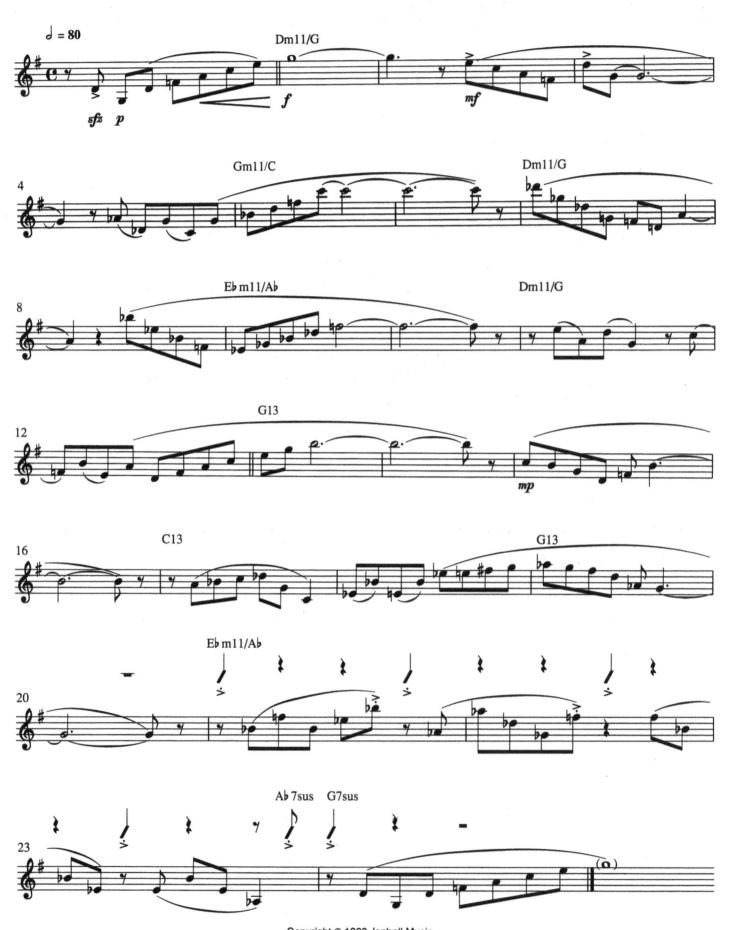

"Cross Court" - Explored

This tune is to be played in octaves with the bass. In my group, bass means Steve LaSpina, who plays the regular upright, acoustic bass with an ease that I much admire. I write a lot of pieces with Steve in mind; challenging things that wouldn't work with just any bass player. Steve always plays them better than I do — with a lot more assurance and throws the challenge right back at me.

I heard "Cross Court" as string bass piece. A blues, it starts rather easily with a perfect 5th and then outlines a G7 with a suspension (Dm over G). On guitar, I use what I imagine a string bass fingering might be, keeping everything on the bottom four strings as much as possible. I think this makes a better ensemble sound.

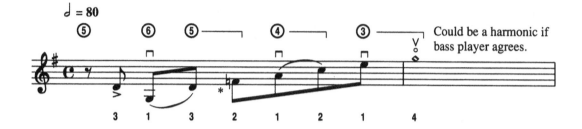

The perfect 5th is a very familiar "bass-sound" and it lies under the hand well on bass and guitar. I decided to exploit this interval (perfect 5th) for the piece.

P5th Intervals

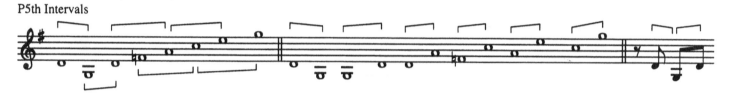

*This crossing under of the 2nd finger (staying on the 5th string) moves the hand up the fingerboard and allows a smooth musical connection. The same can be said for playing A and C on the 4th string with 1st and 2nd fingers although the result isn't as dramatic.

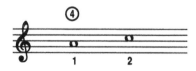

You should feel a "sweep" up the neck and a definite landing on the G, 12th fret. Forward motion is essential in music of any kind.

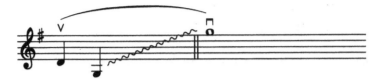

Not dealing with right hand picking for the moment, another interesting fingering is this one:

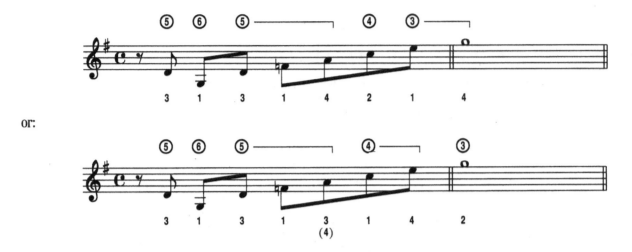

or:

Moving the first finger up from the low G right to the F♮ helps the forward motion even more and helps the left hand get more directly over the work involved. You give yourself more options to move from this position, a good habit to develop for improvising, which involves keeping all options open. The only problem I see with using the first finger on the F♮ is that it has been involved with the low G, whereas the 2nd finger has been hanging around idle, waiting for a chance to get into the action. In either case landing with the 4th finger on G...

...puts you in good shape for the next phrase.

1st Phrase

Back to examining the actual piece as opposed to the guitar fingering, although the two are related. It's filled with 5ths and 3rds, the 5ths overlapping to make 3rds, 7ths, 9ths — an arpeggio.

2nd Phrase

Same idea as phrase 1, only inverted; reinforces G13sus harmony and ends with an open 5th (D-G), an octave above beginning of piece.

3rd Phrase

Again, made up of superimposed 5ths, this time outlining a C9sus which is approached chromatically from Db, a half step above. Also, this phrase is a slight rhythmic displacement of phrase 1, which started with pick-up notes and landed on the root of the G7sus on the downbeat of bar 1. Phrase 3 starts a beat later and doesn't land until one and one half beats into bar 5.

4th Phrase

This is a rhythmic displacement of phrase 2. It approaches G7 with a suggestion of Gb against it. Also, the high Db is dramatic following the high C in bar 6.

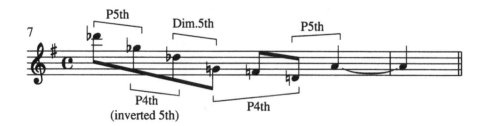

5th Phrase

This phrase starts with an anticipation of the A♭7sus harmony, which is appropriate to bar 9. This creates a little harmonic tension, and once again outlines an E♭m7, arpeggio, with an A♭ bass note implied.

6th Phrase

This phrase outlines G7 with the same downward 5th skips of phrase 1 and moves us into a second blues chorus. The strong note here is the high B, the 3rd of the G7 chord and a major 3rd above the high G in phrase 1. It's also a relief from all the suspended chords.

7th Phrase

A release of tension here (especially for the bass, since we get to drop down an octave) and a rhythmically displaced reference to phase 2.

The bass has quite a bit of just plain physical tension up around B♮, C and D♭ as shown below. The G string is short and tight and the intonation is critical — even dangerous.

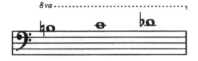

8th Phrase

This phrase takes the half step above and below the root (an earlier idea) and turns it into a C dim scale at 17 and 18. Meanwhile bars 19 and 20 are a reflection of bars 15 and 16. The harmony is G7 —remember this is a blues— and the line flirts with it. It's also the longest phrase of the piece — from bar 17 through bar 20; a total of 4 bars.

9th Phrase

These four bars involve some interplay with the drums, played beautifully by Joey Baron on our recording of "Cross Court." These punctuations are used in bars 21-24 during the solos, too. The harmony here is A♭sus or E♭m7/A♭, and once again the 5th interval is used to outline it. Also a little interest is added by the implied "3" rhythm in bars 21-23.

The drums accent the first of each 3 beats and the guitar and bass start a half beat later and play an eighth note pattern (the pattern is a full beat later at the end of bar 22). Then in bar 24, the whole thing turns around again — back to the 4/4 feeling — and we're again at the top of the 24-bar tune, a double blues. On the recording, the second time through "Cross Court," flügelhornist Tom Harrell improvises in the openings left by the guitar and bass. It makes a nice sounding texture, full of surprises and happy accidents.

After a series of guitar, bass, and flügelhorn solos, Tom and I play two choruses together with just drums accompanying. This leads into an "out chorus" played mostly in unison by flügelhorn and guitar. The flügelhorn has a lovely sound, somewhere between that of a trumpet and a french horn. Its range is the same as a trumpet but, because of its tubing and shape, it has a much softer tone and blends beautifully with the guitar.

"Cross Court" - Out Chorus

"Cross Court" Out Chorus Explored

This 24-plus-bar section, while related to and inspired by the first 24-bar section, brought to mind some musical memories and associations as I was writing it. I thought first of a group led by bassist John Kirby in the 1940s. It featured Billy Kyle (piano), O'Neil Spencer (drums), Buster Bailey (clarinet), Russell Procope (alto sax), and Charlie Shavers, who played trumpet and wrote for the sextet. The arrangements were swinging, tight, elegant, and memorable, evidently, since their sound is still with me. With me too, is the image of the group dressed suavely and appropriately. Whatever happened to that tradition?

Another great small group was Woody Herman's "Woodchoppers," also from the 1940s. Woody had the great Bill Harris on trombone, Sonny Berman or Shorty Rogers on trumpet, Flip Phillips on tenor sax, Jimmy Rowles or Ralph Burns on piano, Billy Bauer or Chuck Wayne on guitar, Chubby Jackson or Joe Mondragon on bass, and various drummers, including Cliff Leeman and the truly magnificent Dave Tough. Woody played clarinet and alto and occasionally sang a tune. The music seemed to have touches of both comedy and deep pathos, with occasional Stravinsky references. Igor Stravinsky had written "Ebony Concerto" for Woody and his full band. Woody's writers, Ralph Burns, Neal Hefti, and Shorty Rogers repaid the compliment. Bars 15, 16, 17 of this "out-chorus" are Stravinsky-like ("Petrouchka," to be exact) and might well have been played by Woody Herman's "Woodchoppers."

Horace Silver writes stunningly for small groups, and I thought of him, too. A list of Horace's famous sidemen would require a book of its own, but Tom Harrell is among them, and somehow the thing has come full circle. Horace Silver's tunes have charm, poignancy, humor, and a strong personal stamp. In other words, they're good. Bill Evans loved them and loved Horace's playing, even though Bill wrote and played quite differently.

Phrase 1 outlines G7 with the 4th suspended and resolved twice:

Again 5ths are outlined:

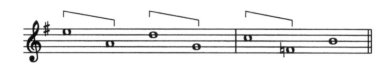

This rhythm is set by these basic melody notes:

Phrase 2 has the same idea as phrase 1 only starting a 5th lower:

The first two phrases are triads outlined:

Phrase 3 is in two parts and is an echo of bars 3 and 4 using B♭ to fit the C7 harmony:

Bar 6 is a quick, rhythmic echo starting on the 2nd eighth note of the first beat.

This sets up a one bar drum fill which really takes up phrase 4:

sfz − p ——————————— mf

Phrase 5 starts with pick up notes in Bar 8 using the triplet motive...

... and climbs up to the 4th of the A♭7 chord in bar 9. More 5ths! The 4th gets resolved to the 3rd in bar 10.

In Phrase 6 the guitar plays a three-voice setting:

The flügelhorn doubles the top part, and the inner voices wobbles from raised 4th to 3rd of G7. This rhythm was suggested in bar 1.

The harmonic spread is carried into the next phrase after the 2-bar drum solo, which is really phrase 7.

Phrase 8 is my sardonic Stravinsky-like phrase:

It was meant to be played with the flügelhorn on the bottom part...

...with the guitar playing the top two lines sounding an 8th lower:

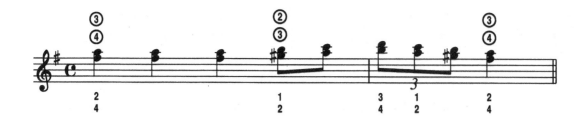

It could also be divided with the melody on the bottom which is easier to finger.

A third solution would be a parallel minor 2nd dissonance instead of a major 7th or minor 9th. Remember, the guitar sounds an octave below where it's written:

15.

Phrase 9 starts with a continuation of the downward motion from bar 16 with the same 3-part voicing (and possible variations) and then reverts back to a bright unison line and another opening for drums at bar 20:

Phrase 10 is a re-run of bars 1 and 2 played a half step higher; above the Ab7 harmony.

It's fun to play phrases 1 and 10 on strings ③, ④ and ⑤. It lends a continuity of sound which is harder to get if one includes string ②:

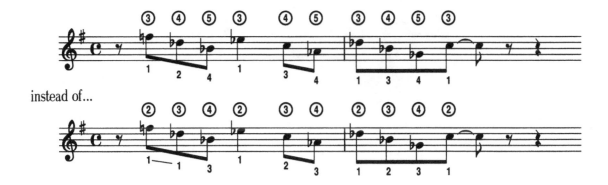

instead of...

As a matter of fact, the entire first ten bars of the 'Out Chorus' could well be played on strings ③, ④, and ⑤. I feel that the sound is more even when wound and unwound strings don't have to be dealt with together. It isn't that thick strings are good and thin strings are bad, it's just that one should be aware of their differences. Also, starting up high on the neck allows the left hand to get aesthetically involved in the rhythmic flow. It feels good, like jogging.

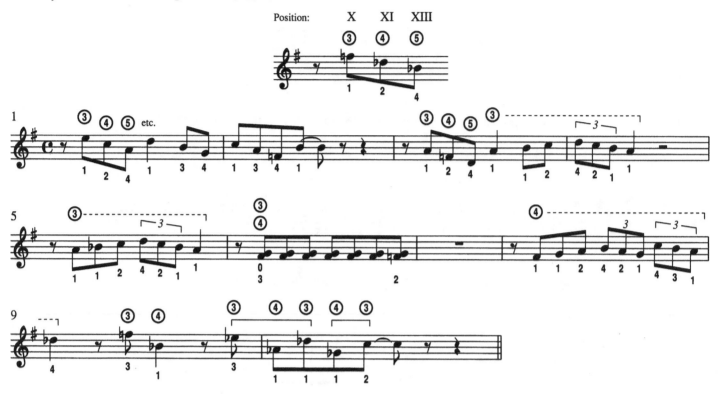

This fingering groups the notes in bar 10 differently. Again, it's a matter of awareness.

Jimmy Giuffre is really keen on the subject of phrasing and articulation. When I worked with him, we spent a lot of time finding fingerings and pickings that would allow the guitar to blend with his clarinet or saxophone, or with Bob Brookmeyer's valve trombone.

One final word on this: bar 8 feels especially nice played entirely on string 4. The left hand gets to do a little Fred Astaire move up the dance floor from F♯ to D♭. Speaking of moves, the great Don Budge, to whom this piece is dedicated, told me that he used to think of music while he was playing a tennis match and hitting his famous backhand cross court shot. Don said the music helped him move on the tennis court. Perhaps thinking of Don Budge and Fred Astaire will help your hand move on the guitar.

Preparation: Village Vanguard

A few years ago, my wife Jane and I took a friend to hear the Pittsburgh Symphony at Lincoln Center in New York. It was exciting for me. Andre Previn, whom I had known in his jazz piano days, was conducting and Yo-Yo Ma, the new star cellist, was to play a concerto.

We had arranged to meet our friend for dinner in a nice restaurant close to the concert. The three of us had a pleasant, leisurely meal with lots of conversation and laughter. Afterward we strolled over to Lincoln Center; a perfect evening, so far.

It was about forty-five minutes before starting time and I thought I would go backstage to leave a hello-note for Previn. At the artists' entrance was a security guard seated at a desk above which were several closed-circuit T.V. screens. On one of these I could see the stage. Andre Previn, Yo-Yo Ma, and the Pittsburgh Symphony were still rehearsing — right up to doors-open time! This made quite an impression on me, especially since I knew the orchestra was leaving by bus for Pittsburgh right after the concert and must have put in quite a full day already. I guess I had imagined that these people, these stars, were exempt from the things that the rest of us working musicians had to go through: road weariness, no food, frantic rehearsing, etc. Surely people this prominent were beyond all of this and lived in a world of tuxedos and champagne.

It was a good lesson for me and I used it a few weeks later. I had booked a week at the Village Vanguard with a new quartet. Actually this was my familiar trio (Terry Clarke on drums and Steve LaSpina on bass) plus Gil Goldstein on piano and synthesizer. Gil is extremely gifted and I figured, rightly, that his tasty use of synthesizer would add a nice new dimension to the group. The only catch was that Terry was in Europe and wouldn't return until the day we opened. Gil, Steve, and I had played together a bit and had worked out some new music of Gil's, plus rearranging some of the old trio stuff. Our only chance to get together as a quartet was to be the sound-check at the Vanguard in the late afternoon of our opening night.

In other words, here was a Jim Hall quartet that had never played together, was due to appear at the famous Village Vanguard, and would have only one quick rehearsal to make it work. What to do?

First, I had to arrive at the sound-check with a clear rehearsal plan, knowing which pieces and parts of pieces needed to be looked at and which ones would fly by themselves with no rehearsal. I needed a rehearsal sequence, being careful not to use up too much time on any one thing. It was important not to put too much pressure on any one musician and not let my criticisms get personal, keeping it light and funny, if possible. I wanted to make Gil feel welcome and equal, while still acknowledging the seniority of the other two members. As you can see, a lot of this has to do with morale boosting, as well as music fixing. If the musicians feel comfortable and relaxed, the music will often fix itself.

Second, I needed a checklist for setting up. Which instruments would go where? Could everyone see each other? Could everyone hear each other? Would we need monitor speakers? Was the soundperson trustworthy? Would he or she change the sound from what was agreed upon once we started to play? This happens a lot, especially on one-night concert tours, and it's very frustrating. Sound engineers may have a completely different idea of how your music should sound from what you do. Often they've come from a rock-and-roll or fusion background and don't realize that jazz needs very little electronic assistance. We make our own dynamics. Once you've started the performance, however, you're in the hands of the engineers, so you'd best be in agreement beforehand. Phil Woods and his group got so fed up with being wiped out by electronics that they now play almost completely acoustically (no microphones) whenever possible.

At times, setting up can take forever, depending on acoustics and attitudes. Most places one plays don't sound good immediately and take half a concert or half a week to get used to. The trick is to recognize this and get on with it, especially when time is limited.

At the Village Vanguard all of this worked out. We set up, rehearsed, had something to eat, and played the opening night. We may have not sounded like the Pittsburgh Symphony, but some people showed up to hear us. We didn't even have to drive to Pittsburgh afterward.

The Village Vanguard holds many special memories and feelings for me. I knew Max Gordon, its colorful owner, for thirty years, which is how long I've played there and gone to hear others play there. I watched Bill Evans record there with Scott LaFaro and Paul Motian. I worked there with Lee Konitz as a duo opposite Miles Davis. Comedian Irwin Corey was at the Vanguard when I played there with Jimmy Giuffre. Mort Sahl, Mike Nichols and Elaine May, Jack Teagarden, Ben Webster, Oscar Peterson...on and on. Lots of good stuff. Lots of photographs on the wall of great musicians, singers, and performers who've been associated with the club.

All of this adds a certain quality to the experience; you really want things to be good.

The Vanguard is a small room; intimate, but with a possibly noisy bar area near the door. It does have a new sound system, which helps, but I hadn't used it at the time of our hurry-up rehearsal.

An ironic footnote....

A Japanese electronics company wanted to capture the acoustics of the Village Vanguard to have on one of its synthesizers as a room sound sample. A couple of their engineers spent quite a while at the club measuring and studying all sorts of things: the kitchen, the ceilings, the height of the raised seating area, etc. In payment for this rather nebulous acquisition, the company gave the Village Vanguard a new sound system, which must have changed everything! I guess what they got was the old Vanguard sound.

Most places today actually seem over-equipped. In fact, most groups seem over amplified and appear to be involved in some sort of macho, electronic arms race. "If you turn the amp up, I'll turn mine up even more!" Roy Eldridge used to refer to my amplifier as "The Third Rail" (like the dangerous rail on a subway track) and he did have a point. Amplifiers can be lethal to music and other living things.

Actually I use my amplifier to play softer, odd as that sounds. With a "good" amp (a subject for a different discussion), I can get a much softer tone quality than I can acoustically -- much less attack, fewer picking noises, more of a legato, saxophone sound.

It isn't that I want to play soft all the time, it's that I want a wide range of volumes — some place to go. "Loud" doesn't mean anything if everything is loud. The same with "soft." These word are meant to compare things; they're meant to be elements of music to use judiciously and not to be worn out. All loud or all soft are equally boring to me.

Speaking of over-equipped places, I once played a concert in a lovely little recital hall in a small town in Italy. The hall was oval-shaped and probably had been used for small presentations, musical comedy, etc. It had beautiful natural acoustics and certainly had been built before punk rock. When we arrived for our sound-check, however, someone had supplied us with on-stage amplification suitable for a soccer stadium. There were two huge banks of speakers hissing away on this tiny stage and looking very grotesque and out of place. It really felt as if this charming old place had been somehow violated and it was very painful to see. One can only imagine the pain of hearing it. Once it was all removed, we played the concert with no microphones and everything was fine.

Room acoustics are important. Sound-checks are important. How big is the room? How high is the ceiling? Will I want to play fewer notes to allow for echo-time? How far back will people be sitting or standing? Will I be able to reach them in every sense of the word? Can I project out as far as the furthest listener — not just with the volume, but with feeling and meaning? Should I be aware of people sitting on the sides or behind me? This is what sound-checks are all about. The actual rehearsing should be done well before this — and usually is, (except in cases like I described at the Village Vanguard) because now is the time to try out different tempos and volumes and see how they work.

I still have a clear picture memory of Papa Jo Jones walking through the aisles of an empty auditorium before a Basie concert. Every few feet he would stop, clap his hands, listen, and look all around. He wanted to know exactly what was going to happen to those beautiful drum sounds of his once the concert started. No amplifiers for Papa Jo.

Jane

By James S. Hall

"Jane" - Explored

The best features of this piece are probably the bass line and the inner voice--the 5th of the chord rising and falling. The piece has a nice sense of direction to it: it goes through three different keys and has a strong melodic pay-off in bars 36-38.

The high D♮ in bar 37 is two octaves and a diminished 4th above the lowest note in bar 18...

I don't advise singing it. It's probably best played on the guitar or on the piano.

There are also some interesting notation questions in it. For example, whether to write bars 1 through 4 as they appear, or this way:

This way you get the confusion of a C♮ and a D♭ both in bar 2, even though I prefer the way the melody and the inner voice look individually here.

Melodically, the major seventh interval looks and feels better than a diminished octave.

Also this:

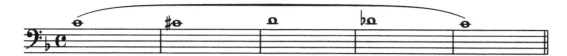

looks and feels better than this:

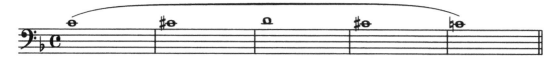

The Db in bar 4 pulls nicely down to the C♮ in bar 5; whereas, a C# in bar 4 looks and feels as if it wants to pull back up to D♮ again. In general, sharps pull upwards and flats push down. However, I decided to avoid the simultaneous C♮ and Db in the melody (bar 2), and to keep the chord spelling (maj 7+5) the same throughout.

"Jane" divides into two sections: Bars 1 through 16 and bars 17 through 44. The first 8 bars of each section are stationary harmonically, while the last 8 bars of the first section and the last 14 bars of the second move upward. I feel good about "Jane" as a composition and also as a musical tribute to my wife, Jane Hall. It's on Concord Records, "The Jim Hall Quartet 'All Across The City' " and features Steve LaSpina on bass, Gil Goldstein on piano, and Terry Clarke on drums. You can judge the results for yourself!

So...What Else Do You Know?

When you walk onto a bandstand, you take your whole self with you. The more of you there is, the better. I've been told that in order to write a book, one must first have something to write about. The same holds true for music: One needs something to play about. Sometimes that involves having sources other than music to draw upon. Sometimes when I need help with music, I put down my guitar and head for the library. Books can be immensely helpful in getting some perspective on music —seeing how it fits in with the other arts, modal music for instance.

My first experience with extensive use of modes in jazz came with hearing Miles Davis' great group in the late 1950s. He had John Coltrane on tenor and soprano sax, Julian Adderley on alto sax, Bill Evans on piano, Paul Chambers on bass, and Philly Joe Jones on drums. A spectacular group of musicians. Fortunately, they recorded enough so that a lot of their great modal experiments are preserved. A quick glance at a music history book, however, tells me that they didn't actually invent the modes. By modes I mean those scales other than major and minor, which are also modes. Nor did G Lydian drift south from Boston in the 1970s. Gregorian chant, sung in the church from at least 600 A.D., contains some of the most stunning, glorious musical moments imaginable. All of the modal possibilities are included somewhere, in some chant, and all are presented in exquisitely shaped single lines. When I was at the Cleveland Institute of Music in the early 1950s, four of us students — including Donald Erb, who's now a prominent composer — spent a year in a special class studying Gregorian chant. We also took a trip to a monastery in Detroit to hear an Easter service sung in Gregorian chant. A couple of years ago, my wife, Jane, and I looked through some churches in Ravenna, Italy, that had lovely intricate mosaics covering the walls. This seemed to round out the modal experience for me. The Gregorian chant was there in those churches, even though no one was singing. Maybe Miles' band was there, too.

As long as I have my library card in hand, I think I'll head toward the literature section: short stories are like good jazz solos, concise and telling. Eudora Welty, James Thurber, John Steinbeck, Edgar Allan Poe; I read them all when I was a kid. Maybe they've already had an effect on my playing. I think I'll re-read them. Good, fun stuff. What about longer forms? My wife loves Toni Morrison's book, "Beloved." I gather it's an impressionistic type novel, sort of like a Turner painting. Why don't I read it and see if Toni Morrison was really influenced by Garcia Marquez when she wrote it? Why don't I re-read Marquez' "A Hundred Years of Solitude" and let both him and Toni Morrison influence me? So what if I'm writing music and they're writing words? Literature and music both have shapes and moods and stories to tell; they're both something done by people to be experienced by other people. Each has to do with self expression and letting others know something about you.

I mentioned J.M.W. Turner's* work in the section on solo construction. In London there's a whole wing of the Tate Museum devoted to Turner's   paintings. What a revelation! What a freeing experience it is to go through that section of the museum and experience his work in sequence. It's freeing in the sense of, "Hey, look what he did here! And look how he developed this in the next painting! Maybe I could do that in my music." Turner's feeling for the sea and its mystery and danger was really quite special. It calls to mind Debussy and Ravel, naturally, but visually, some of his later sea paintings remind me of Willem deKooning. Timeless stuff! Music can also work this way. Elliot Carter's music reminds me of Turner's late works.

Getting back to short stories, this form of writing can be especially useful to a musician, whether a composer or an improviser — a spontaneous composer. Everything is paired down to the essentials, bare bones, almost like a skeleton on which one might later build a novel. The first sentence in a short story is really crucial, meant to get your attention, like the opening phrase of a jazz solo.

Think of the first four bars of Charlie Christian's solo on the blues "Grandslam" with the Benny Goodman sextet:

Now there's an opening sentence! If that doesn't get your attention, nothing will. It got my attention when I first heard it at age thirteen and it has my attention still. I still wonder, "What's he going to do next? What's the next phrase going to be?" Even though I've heard it a thousand times, it's still fresh and provocative.

"He was an old man who fished alone in a skiff in the gulf stream and he had gone eighty-four days now without taking a fish."

Ernest Hemingway—"The Old Man and the Sea"

"Just why it should have happened, or why it should have happened just when it did, he could not, of course, possibly have said; nor perhaps could it even have occurred to him to ask."

Conrad Niven—"Silent Snow, Secret Snow"

"It was almost dawn when young Dr. Phillips swung his sack to his shoulder and left the tide pool."

John Steinbeck—"The Snake"

*Joseph Mallord William Turner (1775-1851, English painter)

Lester Young's opening phrase on "You're Driving Me Crazy"

"Powerhouse is Playing!"

This is from Eudora Welty's short story, "Powerhouse" (1941), which is her Fats Waller fantasy.

These are some of the things that have inspired me and allowed me to develop.

My hope is that, in your search for growth, you'll be as fortunate.

-Jim Hall

JANHALL MUSIC CATALOGUE of Recorded Material

"ALL ACROSS THE CITY" *by James S. Hall*
J. Hall & Zoot Sims ("Two Jims & a Zoot") - Mainstream
Bill Evans & Jim Hall ("Trio/Duo") - Verve
Bill Evans & Jim Hall ("Undercurrent") - Verve
Jim Hall ("All Across The City") - Concord Jazz

"AND I DO" *by James S. Hall*
Jim Hall ("Three") - Concord Jazz

"THE ANSWER IS YES" *by Jane Hall*
Jim Hall ("Concierto") - CTI Records & RCA Canada

"ARUBA" *by James S. Hall*
Jim Hall Trio ("Circles") - Concord Jazz & A&M Canada

"BERMUDA BYE BYE" *by James S. Hall*
Jim Hall ("Commitment") - Horizon & A&M Canada

"BIG BLUES" *by James S. Hall*
Art Farmer/Jim Hall ("Big Blues") - CTI & RCA Canada
Jim Hall/Red Mitchell - Artists House & A&M Canada
Jim Hall ("All Across The City") - Concord Jazz

"BIMINI" *by James S. Hall*
Michael Petrucciani - Blue Note Records

"BLUE DOVE" *by James S. Hall & Red Mitchell*
Jim Hall/Red Mitchell - Artists House & A&M Canada

"BLUE JOE" *by James S. Hall*
Jim Hall ("It's Nice To Be With You")
 - MPS & Pausa Records

"BOTTLENOSE BLUES" *by James S. Hall*
Jim Hall ("Three") - Concord Jazz

"CHORALE AND DANCE" *by James S. Hall*
Jim Hall/Ron Carter ("Telephone")
 - Concord Jazz & A&M Canada

"DOWN FROM ANTIGUA" *by James S. Hall*
Jim Hall Trio ("Circles") - Concord Jazz & A&M Canada

"DOWN THE LINE" *by James S. Hall*
Jim Hall ("Commitment") - Horizon & A&M Canada

"ECHO" *by James S. Hall*
Jim Hall ("Jazz Impressions of Japan") - Horizon

"ERB" *by James S. Hall*
Jim Hall/Lee Konitz ("Duets") - Milestone

"GOODBYE MY LOVE" *by Jane Herbert Hall*
Jim Hall ("Where Would I Be") - Milestone

"HIDE AND SEEK" *by James S. Hall*
Jim Hall ("Three") - Concord Jazz

"IT'S NICE TO BE WITH YOU" *by Jane Herbert Hall*
Jim Hall ("It's Nice To Be With You")
 - MPS & Pausa Records

"KYOTO BELLS" *by James S. Hall*
Jim Hall ("Impressions of Japan")
  - Horizon & A&M Canada

"MINOTAUR" *by James S. Hall*
Jim Hall ("Where Would I Be") - Milestone

"O GATO" *by Jane Herbert Hall*
Jim Hall/Paul Desmond("Bossa Antiqua") - RCA

"OSAKA EXPRESS" a/k/a **"OSAKA"** *by James S. Hall*
Jim Hall/Red Mitchell - Artists House & A&M Canada

"PIECE FOR STRINGS AND GUITAR"
  by James S. Hall
Jim Hall & Gunther Schuller ("Jazz Abstractions")
  - Atlantic

"SIMPLE SAMBA" a/k/a **"SOMBODY'S SAMBA"**
  by James S. Hall
Jim Hall ("Where Would I Be") - Milestone

"SOMETHING TELLS ME" *by Jane Herbert Hall*
Jim Hall ("These Rooms") - Denon
Jim Hall Quartet ("All Across The City") - Concord Jazz

"THREE" *by James S. Hall*
Jim Hall ("Three") - Concord Jazz

"TWISTER" *by Jim Hall and Terry Clarke*
Jim Hall Trio ("Jim Hall Live In Tokyo") - Horizon

"TWO'S BLUES" *by James S. Hall*
Jim Hall ("Concierto") - CTI & A&M Canada
Jim Hall/Ron Carter ("Telephone") - Concord Jazz

"WALK SOFT" *by James S. Hall*
Jim Hall ("Commitment") - Horizon & A&M Canada

"WALTZ NEW" *by James S. Hall*
Jim Hall/Red Mitchell - Artists House & A&M Canada

"WHERE WOULD I BE" *by Jane Herbert Hall*
Jim Hall ("Where Would I Be") - Milestone

"WHOSE BLUES" *by James S. Hall*
Jim Hall/Ron Carter Duo ("Alone Together") - Milestone

"WITHOUT WORDS" *by James S. Hall*
Jim Hall ("Jazz Impressions of Japan")
  - Horizon & A&M Canada
Jim Hall/George Shearing ("First Edition") - Concord Jazz

"YOUNG ONE, FOR DEBRA" *by James S. Hall*
Jim Hall ("It's Nice To Be With You") - MPS & Pausa
Jim Hall Quartet ("All Across The City") - Concord Jazz

ARTIST TRANSCRIPTIONS

Artist Transcriptions are authentic, note-for-note transcriptions of today's hottest artists in jazz, pop and rock. These outstanding, accurate arrangements are in an easy-to-read format which includes all essential lines. Artist Transcriptions can be used to perform, sequence or for reference.

CLARINET
00672423	Buddy De Franco Collection	$19.95

FLUTE
00672379	Eric Dolphy Collection	$19.95
00672582	The Very Best of James Galway	$19.99
00672372	James Moody Collection – Sax and Flute	$19.95

GUITAR & BASS
00660113	Guitar Style of George Benson	$19.99
00672573	Ray Brown – Legendary Jazz Bassist	$22.99
00672331	Ron Carter Collection	$19.99
00660115	Al Di Meola – Friday Night in San Francisco	$17.99
00604043	Al Di Meola – Music, Words, Pictures	$14.95
00125617	Best of Herb Ellis	$19.99
00673245	Jazz Style of Tal Farlow	$24.99
00699306	Jim Hall – Exploring Jazz Guitar	$19.99
00672353	The Joe Pass Collection	$19.99
00673216	John Patitucci	$17.99
00672374	Johnny Smith – Guitar Solos	$24.99
00672320	Mark Whitfield Guitar Collection	$19.95

PIANO & KEYBOARD
00672338	The Monty Alexander Collection	$19.95
00672487	Monty Alexander Plays Standards	$19.95
00672520	Count Basie Collection	$19.95
00192307	Bebop Piano Legends	$19.99
00113680	Blues Piano Legends	$22.99
00672526	The Bill Charlap Collection	$19.99
00278003	A Charlie Brown Christmas	$17.99
00672439	Cyrus Chestnut Collection	$19.95
00672300	Chick Corea – Paint the World	$19.99
00146105	Bill Evans – Alone	$19.99
00672548	The Mastery of Bill Evans	$16.99
00672425	Bill Evans – Piano Interpretations	$22.99
00672365	Bill Evans – Play Standards	$22.99
00121885	Bill Evans – Time Remembered	$19.99
00672510	Bill Evans Trio Vol. 1: 1959-1961	$27.99
00672511	Bill Evans Trio Vol. 2: 1962-1965	$27.99
00672512	Bill Evans Trio Vol. 3: 1968-1974	$29.99
00672513	Bill Evans Trio Vol. 4: 1979-1980	$24.95
00193332	Erroll Garner – Concert by the Sea	$22.99
00672486	Vince Guaraldi Collection	$19.99
00289644	The Definitive Vince Guaraldi	$34.99
00672419	Herbie Hancock Collection	$22.99
00672438	Hampton Hawes Collection	$19.95

00672322	Ahmad Jamal Collection	$24.99
00255671	Jazz Piano Masterpieces	$19.99
00124367	Jazz Piano Masters Play Rodgers & Hammerstein	$19.99
00672564	Best of Jeff Lorber	$19.99
00672476	Brad Mehldau Collection	$22.99
00672388	Best of Thelonious Monk	$22.99
00672389	Thelonious Monk Collection	$24.99
00672390	Thelonious Monk Plays Jazz Standards – Volume 1	$22.99
00672391	Thelonious Monk Plays Jazz Standards – Volume 2	$22.99
00672433	Jelly Roll Morton – The Piano Rolls	$17.99
00672553	Charlie Parker Piano featuring The Paul Smith Trio (Book/CD)	$19.95
00264094	Oscar Peterson – Night Train	$19.99
00672544	Oscar Peterson – Originals	$14.99
00672531	Oscar Peterson – Plays Duke Ellington	$24.99
00672563	Oscar Peterson – A Royal Wedding Suite	$19.99
00672569	Oscar Peterson – Tracks	$19.99
00672533	Oscar Peterson – Trios	$29.99
00672534	Very Best of Oscar Peterson	$22.95
00672371	Bud Powell Classics	$22.99
00672376	Bud Powell Collection	$24.99
00672507	Gonzalo Rubalcaba Collection	$19.95
00672303	Horace Silver Collection	$24.99
00672316	Art Tatum Collection	$24.99
00672355	Art Tatum Solo Book	$19.99
00672357	The Billy Taylor Collection	$24.95
00673215	McCoy Tyner	$22.99
00672321	Cedar Walton Collection	$19.95
00672519	Kenny Werner Collection	$19.95
00672434	Teddy Wilson Collection	$22.99

SAXOPHONE
00672566	The Mindi Abair Collection	$14.99
00673244	Julian "Cannonball" Adderley Collection	$22.99
00673237	Michael Brecker	$19.99
00672429	Michael Brecker Collection	$24.99
00672394	James Carter Collection	$19.95
00672529	John Coltrane – Giant Steps	$17.99
00672494	John Coltrane – A Love Supreme	$16.99
00672493	John Coltrane Plays "Coltrane Changes"	$19.95
00672453	John Coltrane Plays Standards	$24.99
00673233	John Coltrane Solos	$27.99
00672328	Paul Desmond Collection	$19.99
00672530	Kenny Garrett Collection	$22.99

00699375	Stan Getz	$19.99
00672377	Stan Getz – Bossa Novas	$22.99
00672375	Stan Getz – Standards	$19.99
00673254	Great Tenor Sax Solos	$22.99
00672523	Coleman Hawkins Collection	$22.99
00672330	Best of Joe Henderson	$24.99
00673239	Best of Kenny G	$22.99
00673229	Kenny G – Breathless	$19.99
00672462	Kenny G – Classics in the Key of G	$22.99
00672485	Kenny G – Faith: A Holiday Album	$17.99
00672373	Kenny G – The Moment	$19.99
00672498	Jackie McLean Collection	$19.95
00672372	James Moody Collection – Sax and Flute	$19.95
00672416	Frank Morgan Collection	$19.95
00672539	Gerry Mulligan Collection	$22.99
00672561	Best of Sonny Rollins	$19.95
00102751	Sonny Rollins, Art Blakey & Kenny Drew with the Modern Jazz Quartet	$17.95
00675000	David Sanborn Collection	$19.99
00672528	The Bud Shank Collection	$19.95
00672491	The New Best of Wayne Shorter	$24.99
00672550	The Sonny Stitt Collection	$19.95
00672524	Lester Young Collection	$19.99

TROMBONE
00672332	J.J. Johnson Collection	$22.99
00672489	Steve Turré Collection	$19.99

TRUMPET
00672557	Herb Alpert Collection	$19.99
00672480	Louis Armstrong Collection	$19.99
00672481	Louis Armstrong Plays Standards	$19.99
00672435	Chet Baker Collection	$22.99
00672556	Best of Chris Botti	$19.99
00672448	Miles Davis – Originals, Vol. 1	$19.99
00672451	Miles Davis – Originals, Vol. 2	$19.95
00672449	Miles Davis – Standards, Vol. 2	$19.95
00672479	Dizzy Gillespie Collection	$19.95
00673214	Freddie Hubbard	$19.99
00672506	Chuck Mangione Collection	$19.99
00672525	Arturo Sandoval – Trumpet Evolution	$19.99

HAL•LEONARD®